NEW CATHAY

新华夏集　当代中国诗选

Tupelo Press Poetry in Translation

Abiding Places: Korea, South and North, by Ko Un
Translated from Korean by
Hillel Schwartz and Sunny Jung

Invitation to a Secret Feast: Selected Poems, by Joumana Haddad
Translated from Arabic by Khaled Mattawa
with Najib Awad, Issa Boullata, Marilyn Hacker,
Joumana Haddad, Henry Matthews,
and David Harsent

Night, Fish and Charlie Parker, by Phan Nhien Hao
Translated from Vietnamese by Linh Dinh

Stone Lyre: Poems of René Char
Translated from French
by Nancy Naomi Carlson

This Lamentable City: Poems of Polina Barskova
Translated from Russian by
Ilya Kaminsky with Katie Farris,
Rachel Galvin, and Matthew Zapruder

New Cathay: Contemporary Chinese Poetry
Edited by Ming Di and translated from Chinese by
Neil Aitken, Katie Farris, Ming Di, Christopher Lupke,
Tony Barnstone, Nick Admussen, Jonathan Stalling,
Afaa M. Weaver, Eleanor Goodman, Ao Wang, Dian Li,
Kerry Shawn Keys, Jennifer Kronovet,
Elizabeth Reitzell, and Cody Reese

Ex-Voto: Poems of Adélia Prado
Translated from Portuguese
by Ellen Doré Watson

新华夏集 当代中国诗选

NEW CATHAY

Contemporary Chinese Poetry

Edited by
Ming Di

Translated from Chinese by
Neil Aitken, Katie Farris,
Ming Di, Christopher Lupke,
Tony Barnstone, Nick Admussen,
Jonathan Stalling, Afaa M. Weaver,
Eleanor Goodman, Ao Wang,
Dian Li, Kerry Shawn Keys,
Jennifer Kronovet,
Elizabeth Reitzell,
and Cody Reese

Tupelo Press
North Adams, Massachusetts

New Cathay: Contemporary Chinese Poetry
Compilation copyright 2013 Ming Di and Tupelo Press.
Translations copyrighted by the authors and/or translators.
All poems in this anthology are new translations except for the following, which have
appeared in journals in earlier versions, translated as indicated: Zheng Xiaoqiong's
"Industrial Zone" (Jonathan Stalling) in *Chinese Literature Today;* Zang Di's
"In Memory of Wittgenstein" (Ming Di and Neil Aitken), Lü De'an's "Offenders" (Ming Di),
Ya Shi's "Cryptic Poem" (Nick Admussen), Sun Wenbo's "Bland Life, Blunt Poetry"
(Ming Di and Neil Aitken), and Qiu Qixun's "Song of Love" (Ming Di) in *Poetry
International;* and Yang Xiaobin's "The Clay Pot of Tennessee" (Neil Aitken and Ming Di
with the author), Mai Mang's "In My Lifetime... " (the author), and Jiang Hao's "The
Shape of the Ocean" (Ming Di and Afaa M. Weaver) in *Poetry East West.*
The following poems were featured in the Poetry Foundation's Poetics of Six Continents
program: Lü De'an's "Offenders," Zang Di's "Association of How to Conditionally Grasp the
Truth" and "In Memory of Paul Klee, A Book Series," Duo Duo's "Morning" and
"The River of Amsterdam," Jiang Hao's "The Shape of the Ocean," Lan Lan's "Wind,"
Jiang Li's "An Old Woman's Timepiece" and "Eternity," Ya Shi's "Cryptic Poem,"
Sun Wenbo's "Poetry of Nonsense," and Hu Xudong's "Mama Ana Paula also Writes Poetry."

Library of Congress Cataloging-in-Publication Data

New Cathay : contemporary Chinese poetry 1990-2012 / edited by Ming Di. -- First edition.
pages   cm
ISBN 978-1-936797-24-0 (pbk. : alk. paper)
1. Chinese poetry--20th century--Translations into English. 2. Chinese poetry--21st century--
Translations into English. I. Ming Di (Poet) editor of compilation.
PL2658.E3N45 2013
895.1'1008--dc23

2013011206

First edition: May 2013.

Cover and text designed by Josef Beery.
Cover art: Xiaoze Xie, "April–May 2000, Shanghai #1," 2001, oil on canvas, 45 x 64 inches. From
the series of "Amplified Moments." Used courtesy of the artist and
Chambers Fine Art, New York (http://chambersfineart.com/).

Tupelo Press
P.O. Box 1767, North Adams, Massachusetts 01247
Telephone: (413) 664–9611
editor@tupelopress.org / www.tupelopress.org

Tupelo Press is an award-winning independent literary press that publishes fine fiction, nonfic-
tion, and poetry in books that are a joy to hold as well as read. Tupelo Press is a registered
501(c)3 nonprofit organization, and we rely on public support to carry out our mission of
publishing extraordinary work that may be outside the realm of large commercial publishers.
Financial donations are welcome and are tax deductible.

Published with the support of the National Endowment for the Arts and as part of the Poets in
the World series created by the Harriet Monroe Poetry Institute at the Poetry Foundation.

ART WORKS.
arts.gov

This book is part of the Poets in the World series created by

THE HARRIET MONROE
POETRY INSTITUTE

The Harriet Monroe Poetry Institute is an independent forum
created by the Poetry Foundation to provide a space in which fresh
thinking about poetry, in both its intellectual and its practical needs,
can flourish free of any allegiance other than to the best ideas. The
Institute convenes leading poets, scholars, publishers, educators, and
other thinkers from inside and outside the poetry world to address
issues of importance to the art form of poetry and to identify and
champion solutions for the benefit of the art.

Visit www.poetry foundation.org/foundation/poetryinstitute.

The Poetry Foundation, publisher of *Poetry* magazine, is an
independent literary organization committed to a vigorous
presence for poetry in our culture. It exists to discover and
celebrate the best poetry and to place it before the largest possible
audience. The Poetry Foundation seeks to be a leader in shaping a
receptive climate for poetry by developing new audiences, creating
new avenues for delivery, and encouraging new kinds of poetry
through innovative partnerships, prizes, and programs.

For more information, visit www.poetryfoundation.org.

Contents

EDITOR'S INTERVIEWS AND SURVEYS

EDITOR'S INTERVIEWS WITH POETS (EXCERPTS)

PREFACE: 1990, THE COMING OF A SILVER AGE

Over the course of three thousand years of Chinese poetry, tremendous changes have taken place, especially in 1917, the year that breaks Chinese poetry into two worlds: classical and modern. Yet in the past two decades, poets in China have been trying, after many years of influence from the West, to "return" to ancient literary traditions. However, this burgeoning renaissance doesn't mean to write exactly the way poetry was written in the distant past, but to re-explore the legacy of the breadth of Chinese literature and to adopt a classical "spirit" in perspectives and emotional appeals. What makes the story more complicated is that there are many different eras and modes to which contemporary Chinese poets may try to return. Some see exemplars in the Tang or Song dynasties, and some prefer the poetry of Chu, whereas others admire the simplicity and lively cadences in the *Book of Songs*, a gathering of poems from the eleventh to sixth century BCE, the first Chinese anthology.

While poetry from the Tang dynasty (about 618–907 CE) has been introduced into English through translations in great abundance, there has been little translation of the poetry by Qu Yuan (343–278 BCE), from the State of Chu, the first known poet of ancient China. Likewise, there have been numerous translations of what is called "Misty" poetry (since the 1970s) and Post-Misty poetry (since the mid-1980s), but other approaches outside the Misty/Post-Misty trends have barely been introduced, and certainly not in depth, with genuinely poetic presentations.

This anthology therefore focuses on non-Misty poetry, zooming in on the past two decades. While some of the poets featured here started writing as early as the 1970s, none of them were formally associated with the Misty group. For instance, in an interview with poet-journalist Ling Yue in 2004, Duo Duo said firmly, "I have never been Misty." Many of the non-Misty poets have been influenced by classical Chinese poetry as well as by Western literature, and many younger poets have bypassed the Misty poetry and taken the ancients Qu Yuan, Du Fu, and Tao Yuan-ming or modern poets Bian Zhilin and Mu Dan from the 1940s as their literary ancestors.

"NEW POETRY"

Over the past decade, there have been vigorous discussions and passionate debates in China about "One Hundred Years of Chinese New Poetry," and many questions have been raised, such as "Where is Chinese poetry going?" "Is our poetry getting better or worse?" and "Have we accomplished glorious achievements, like the poets in the Tang dynasty?" Meanwhile, some Western observers have asserted that Chinese contemporary poets have not made the best use of their own traditions.

The New Poetry in China is approximately parallel with literary modernism in Europe and North America. When Ezra Pound and T. S. Eliot, young free spirits from America, were experimenting with imagery and poetic language in resistance to what they perceived as the deadening Victorian and Georgian styles, the first generation of New Poetry in China employed "plain speech" (or vernacular language) in writing, attempting to wipe out the bookish language of the Qing dynasty (1644–1912) and Ming dynasty (1368–1644).

1912 saw the overthrow of the last dynasty and the birth of the Republic of China. In 1915, when Ezra Pound published his book *Cathay* featuring some versions of classical Chinese poems, Chinese intellectuals were wholeheartedly promoting Western philosophies. In 1917, when T. S. Eliot published *Prufrock and Other Observations* in London, Hu Shi (1891–1962) returned to China to teach at Beijing (Peking) University after finishing graduate studies in the United States, and he published eight "free verse" poems that year to promote new thoughts and new language, which marks the beginning of New Poetry in China — a mixed lineage from the very beginning. However, the classical literature and the classical Chinese philosophies Confucianism and Daoism were never abandoned completely but were resurrected again and again throughout the modern and contemporary periods in China.

Although not the best poet of his time, Hu Shi is generally considered to be China's pioneer modernist, and his *Experiment* (1920) was the first collection of free verse published in China. During the following decades many new poets appeared. Xu Zhimo (1897–1931) studied in the United States and England before returning to China in 1922, when he started the weekly "Modern Review" with Hu Shi and acted as a translator for Indian poet Rabindranath Tagore, who visited China in 1924. Xu went to Europe in 1925 and returned to China again in 1927 to found the "New Moon" school of poetry. In his short life span, he introduced a broader variety of English poetry to China, including Thomas Hardy as well as the Romanticists. Wen Yiduo (1899–1946) went to the University of Chicago to study art, then returned to China in 1925 and became an important member of the New Moon school. Li Jinfa (1900–1976) studied in France and brought French Symbolism to China when he published his first poetry book in 1925.

Chinese modernism evolved from the New Moon and Symbolist schools and matured around 1935, with Dai Wangshu (1905–1950) and Bian Zhilin (1910–2000) as leading poets. Other notables include Mu Dan (1918–1977) and Zheng Min (1920–), who both returned to China after graduate studies in the United States. Ai Qing (1910–1996), father of the internationally renowned dissident artist Ai Weiwei (1957–), was a work-study student of art in the late 1920s in France, where he was exposed to European modernism, and after coming home in 1932 he became a leading poet in China. Feng Zhi (1905–1993) went to study in Germany in 1930, and after returning to China he translated Rilke's poetry. The majority of the first generation of New Poetry were poet-translators, and they not only brought Western literature to China but made great contributions to the development of China's own poetics.

After the People's Republic of China was founded in 1949, doors to the West were closed, and an officially sanctioned poetry for "serving the people" prevailed in mainland China for twenty years, while in the 1950s and 1960s poets such as Luo Fu (1928–) and Ya Xuan (1932–) carried on in the modernist mode in Taiwan (and later, in Canada), and Ji Xian (1913–) continued to write as a Chinese modernist after moving to the United States.

In 1976 another era began in mainland China, represented by the work of Bei Dao, Jiang He, Shu Ting, Gu Cheng, and Yang

Lian, who were again emulating the early modernist poetry of the West. These poets were tagged with the term "Misty" by critics in the 1980s; the poets themselves preferred to be called the "Today Group," acknowledging the role of the journal "Today" (founded in 1978 by Bei Dao and Mang Ke) in gathering together many underground poets of that time.

In the mid-1980s, a "third generation" of poets arose in revolt, mocking the lofty tone and lyricism of Misty poetry and promoting instead the use of "spoken language" in contrast with "misty" expressions. Around the same time, feminist poetry became popular, echoing the American female confessional poems that were being introduced through translation. Despite their alternative stance, both the spoken language and feminist poetries bore striking resemblance to Misty poetry, especially the latter in its continuation of a fighting posture against "patriarchal society." The protest carnival did not last long. Except for a few who have continued writing interesting poems, most of the Misty and Post-Misty poets have either stopped writing poetry or have not produced particularly significant or innovative work.

Real changes took place quietly in the 1990s, when poets such as Zhang Shuguang, Sun Wenbo, and Xiao Kaiyu promoted narrative features in poetry, and Zang Di advocated anti-sentimentality, questioning the manner in which Chinese poetry had long been composed. Instead of attacking recent trends, these 1990s innovators ignored the Misty poetry. They re-discovered poets from the 1940s (as T. S. Eliot had re-discovered the metaphysical poets). There was no name for their counter-movement, but in 1999, they (and others, including Xi Chuan and Wang Jiaxin) were accused by the spoken language group of being "poets of intellectual writing," which for many years had been a derogatory epithet, and as a result these poets have been underrepresented in studies of Chinese poetry. And yet it is this spirit of "intellectual writing" that has been growing in the past twenty years, steadily and forcefully, and this is what has transformed the landscape of contemporary Chinese poetry.

LANGUAGE AND FORM

In 1917, the year that Hu Shi introduced free verse to China, T. S. Eliot published his essay "Reflections on *Vers Libre*," where he argued that "*vers libre* does not exist," because "there is no freedom in art..." Contemporary Chinese poets believe that each poem has its own form.

When Hu Shi promoted free verse as a revolution against the old restraints, he emphasized that "free" would mean a way of writing poetry in contrast with a "classical" way of using rhymes and a strict tonal system. Hu Shi's first example of free verse was a short essay with line breaks, and his focus was on plain speech or vernacular language. His practice was more of a manifestation than an artistic success.

In the following decades, the New Moon School promoted a sort of "regulated" verse. Wen Yiduo studied and practiced classical forms before and after his stay in the United States, and he formulated theories for a new "form" of writing. If he had not been killed by nationalists in 1946, Chinese poetry might have shifted gears. Around this time, Feng Zhi experimented with Chinese sonnets; Mu Dan explored new syntax and new musicality in free verse writing.

Misty poetry began after the Mao era in China as a rebellion against the established political system and ideologies. These poets won enormous fame internationally, but they did not go far in terms of language innovation or construction of poetics.

In 1994, Chinese poet Zang Di published a groundbreaking essay, "Post-Misty, as a Way of Poetry Writing," in which he defined 1984 as the end of Misty domination, asserting the significance of new poetic approaches. At the same time he tactfully pointed out certain limitations of the Post-Misty poetry of the late 1980s.

I agree with Zang Di and many other poets in using Post-Misty as a term for the "third generation." Furthermore, I use this term to include the spoken language, "Them," "Not Not," feminist poetry, and all of those trends or schools that made a big show in the late 1980s. Other people have used Post-Misty to include everyone in China who started writing poetry after the 1970s, but this extended use of the term is misleading and gives the impression that the writing of free verse began with the Misty group in 1970s. In actuality contemporary Chinese poets have rediscovered the achievements of 1930s and 1940s New Poetry, which originated in 1917. Considering almost a century of Chinese New Poetry, Misty is but a small period. In the newly published thirty-volume "One Hundred Year Canon of New Poetry," Pre-Misty and Misty poets occupy only one volume, and Post-Misty poems are scattered around, no longer a coherent or vital force. A large number of strong non-Misty poets from the 1949–79 era have been rediscovered and presented in this "Canon" and in other recent anthologies. Many contemporary poets believe that poetry in the 1970s and 1980s has been overrated.

The Misty poets may have succeeded politically and socially, but their poetry resembles the poetry of the Mao era in adopting the dualism of simplistic "black and white." Likewise, Post-Misty poetry shows similarities to Misty in its preponderance of oppositional postures.

And viewed from today's vantage, Post-Misty shows strong similarities to Misty even aesthetically. If poetry is "*clear expression* of mixed feelings" (as W. H. Auden said), this is what we see: Misty poetry used misty or obscure language to convey one-dimensional messages; Post-Misty used clear language to convey one-dimensional messages. The generation of the 1990s, however, uses clear and current language (spoken and written) to convey multiple layers of meanings.

It is the non-spoken language poets such as Zang Di, Ya Shi, and Hu Xudong who tend to pick up dynamic jargons from the streets or mass media and blend them into unusual syntax, which has infused new vigor into contemporary poetry. It is also the non-spoken language poets who have made more extensive use of classical literature and given that tradition new life. For instance, Duo Duo's repetition of adverbials is a re-creation of repeated patterns in ancient poetry. Xiao Kaiyu and Jiang Hao frequently turn to classical literature for dictions, tones, and moods — or to be recharged.

Critics have tried for many years to compare Duo Duo and Wang Xiaoni with the Misty poets, and tried to analyze the differences. I would simply take these poets out of the "Misty" mislabeling. I would group them together with poets who started writing in the 1980s but became mature in the 1990s, including Zhang Shuguang, Sun Wenbo, Xiao Kaiyu, Zang Di, and others, along with poets who started writing in the 1990s, such as Jiang Hao, Jiang Tao and Hu Xudong. They are neither Misty or Post-Misty, but good poets.

An interesting yet ironic phenomenon in the history of contemporary Chinese poetry is that the Misty and Post-Misty poetries were never really all that opaque — they had a clear target to shoot at, government and society. By contrast, the poets of the 1990s and beyond have never been called misty or obscure, as their writings seem transparent, yet true intensions are elusive. For instance, critics have failed to explain what Zang Di was trying to say in one of his earlier poems:

Room with a Plum Tree

There was a moment after all
when the woman in the room was young
standing still before the window of April
On her slim shoulders landed two white pigeons

But perhaps there were no pigeons
It was her branching body
that made us feel the dew-wet tranquility
and hot intestines sprouting from her intense veins

Like stars the plum tree bloomed full
illuminating her face with its first flowering
and through her glowing gaze
framed the bluest mystery in that room

房屋与梅树

毕竟存在过那样的时刻
房间里的女人还很年轻
她站立不动在四月的窗前
瘦削的双肩栖落两只白鸽

其实很可能并没有白鸽
而是她那花枝般的姿态
让我们感到露水滋润的安宁
血液凝结就像暗红的辣肠

那些梅花繁星般饱满
把春天最初的盛开移近她的面庞
甚至通过她鲜明的凝神注目
构成那房间里最深湛的秘密

(1984)

Poets and critics saw immediately that this kind of writing was different from Misty or Post-Misty. Here poetry was no longer being used as a political or social tool; not as protest, but with fascination, or an obsession with the inner structures of things in contrast with outer appearances. Yet many were puzzled as to what this "she" represents. A woman or a tree? Mother or girl friend? Muse? Or poetic form itself? The ambiguity and multiple potentials, the clear and elegant language, the fusion of classical imagery (plum tree and white pigeons) with contemporary experience, and the wild imagination (branching body) — these qualities made people bewildered. Zang Di's poetry evolved in the early 1990s and became illusionary and difficult. Call this "intellectual" or "academic" writing if you don't understand its mechanism. That is what the proponents of "spoken language" were doing: attacking poets whose subtleties were hard to comprehend.

In Xiao Kaiyu's poem "Mao Zedong" (1987), included in this anthology, the emotion was not easy to grasp and the language was classical-sounding and tricky. Xiao Kaiyu in the south and Zang Di in the north were hailed as innovators by a small number of poets in China. Like Duo Duo, Zhang Shuguang, Song Lin, and Lü De'an, who also remained in the shadows for many years, Xiao Kaiyu and Zang Di were so private that most readers in China hardly heard of them in the 1980s and early 1990s. They emerged as mature poets in mid-1990s, ten years after other poets of their generation won acclaim in the 1980s. Yet the solid craftsmanship and pioneer spirit of the 1990s poets in "making it new" have influenced more and more poets in contemporary China. What's new about their poetry is a complexity that had never been seen before in the history of New Poetry, and an innovative syntax that marked the 1990s as a new age — poetry became more poetic when empowered by the use of prose language. Zang Di introduced phrases like "after all," "therefore," "as a result," "in fact," "even though," "nevertheless," and "furthermore" into poetry, making the ordinary and the old sound fresh. This solved problems of language, by loosening up the rigid structures of Misty poetry and tightening up the sloppy structure (or no structure) of Post-Misty. Xiao Kaiyu and Sun Wenbo have supported completeness in thought, in logic, and in sentences, as opposed to the fragmentation often seen in Misty and Post-Misty writing. But even more important than their linguistic innovation is the profound emotion of these poets, combined with an intellectual acuity that's presented beautifully and subtly.

Many of the poets selected for *New Cathay* come from the "intellectual" contingent, but readers will also find in the poems featured here other styles and approaches. What these poets share is that they've drawn upon a variety of Western trends and also sought to revitalize Chinese traditions, aiming to reinvigorate the New Poetry that originated a century ago.

"Chinese-ness"

The subtitle of this anthology doesn't use "Chinese" to refer only to a geographical area or to poetry written in Chinese language (there is more than one language in China), but to a character-istic "Chinese-ness" that traces back to ancient traditions. I will not define what Chinese-ness is, but invite readers to discover its range in meaning by reading through the anthology. This gathering makes an argument that Chinese poems in the past twenty years have been restoring a great legacy, yet in individual ways.

Fragmented sentences and run-on lines are two of the most obvious features Chinese poets learned and over-imitated from the West or Western translations of Chinese classical poetry. The earlier attempt to return to Chinese-ness involved maintaining "complete-ness" in each line and "wholeness" in each quatrain, as exemplified in the poem "Room with a Plum Tree," which has some enjambed lines, which vary the rhythm.

The poets presented here can't be easily categorized according to superficially defined "schools" or "movements"; they do show, poet after poet, tremendously varied forms of sensitivity and con-sciousness, and different ways of reacting to the surrounding world. And in addition to offering a variety of voices in this anthology, I've interviewed many of the poets and translated some of their answers here, to let them speak directly to readers about what has happened in China since 1990 and about how they view their tradi-tions and Western influences. These interviews illuminate the time periods through which the poets have lived, serving as comple-mentary introductions to their poems.

Some have criticized Chinese contemporary poets for being too "Westernized" and lacking uniqueness. It is true that poets can be most curious about what is most far away. The Indian poet Tagore didn't leave long-lasting impressions or influences in China, even though he put his footsteps in the country and was well received. It is the "unfamiliar ghosts" of Europe and America that have haunted Chinese poets the most — the imagination of the "Other." And this has been mutual. T. S. Eliot, who influenced Chinese poets to an enormous degree, was influenced by Baudelaire, who in turn had been influenced by Li Bai. Twentieth-century American poetry has likewise been filled with "Oriental" allusions and imagery and with the stylistic influences of ancient Chinese nature poetry. Chinese poets recognize their own blood coursing through the bodies of others.

Several authors featured here say in the accompanying interviews that they are not afraid of losing an "individual voice," emphasizing that they welcome influences and interactions. As Zang Di says, "Chinese New Poetry started with Walt Whitman inhabiting Bian Zhilin's body." Wang Jiaxin, Hu Xudong, and others have built personal aesthetics and kinship through translating foreign poetry. And the young poet Jiang Li predicts that "the Chinese–Western fusion will be an important part of Chinese poetry in the years to come." These poets choose in their writings to have a dialogue with poets from other countries and eras. If Shakespeare could write about old Danish legends, why can't Chinese poets write about American or Spanish stories? The resulting "foreignness" can make their poetry even more Chinese. Or, to reverse the cliché: the more international, the more local. Or to borrow T. S. Eliot's phrase, the division between classical poetry and New Poetry does not exist: there is only good poetry, bad poetry, and chaos.

Like the poet-translators from the 1920s to 1940s, many contemporary Chinese poets view translation as part of their own creative writing. If Ezra Pound "re-invented" Chinese poetry, they have re-invented English, French, German, Russian, Arabic, Spanish, Portuguese poetry — you name it.

I don't want to seem to over-defend the poets in my home country, but I do want to point out that they've inherited many reputedly "foreign" features from the homemade classical literature. A poem seemingly in Robert Frost's style may revive Tao Yuanming or Wang Wei. A poem of dramatic monologue that appears to copy Robert Browning or T. S. Eliot but actually follow ancient poems such as "Chang Gan Xing" (or "River Merchant's Wife: A Letter"). Narrative forms may look like they've been learned from Anglo-American poetry, but tell me which poem from the *Book of Songs* isn't narrative?

From emulating Western poetry in the 1970s and 1980s, to blending the Western-Chinese modes and expanding the boundaries of poetic expressions in the 1990s and twenty-first century, Chinese poetry has been progressing artistically as well as linguistically.

It is for the aesthetic vitality and maturity of Chinese poetry since 1990 that this period may be considered a Silver Age, as we perceive the time of the *Book of Songs* as a Bronze Age and the Tang Dynasty as a Golden Age. Personally I find the past two decades more interesting than even the high Tang, but to call this a Silver Age is to save room for perfection.

Coincidentally or not, many of the contemporary Chinese poets take the Russian poets of the Silver Age as their kin and soul mates. Mandelstam, Tsvetaeva, Akhmatova, and Pasternak did not belong to any school or faction, and together their works comprised a Silver Age achievement. Similarly, Duo Duo, Zang Di, Xiao Kaiyu, Zhang Shuguang, Sun Wenbo, Ya Shi, Jiang Tao, Hu Xutong, and many others do not belong to any school or group either; these are ambitious poets who have made great efforts to change the nature of contemporary Chinese poetry, and through the cumulative impact of their individual writing, we see how Chinese poetry has evolved.

A NOTE ABOUT NAMES

For the spelling of names, we've used the Pinyin system, which was established in 1950s, and the family name is placed before the given name, as is the general practice in China. Some clarifications may be needed; for example Li Po (in Wade-Giles) and Li Bai (in Pinyin) are one person, as is also the case with Tu Fu (in Wade-Giles) and Du Fu (in Pinyin). However Jiang Tao, Jiang Hao, and Jiang Li in this anthology have completely different family names, although they look the same in the Romanized Pinyin system; therefore the poets' Chinese names are given in the table of contents and the headings for each introduction.

HISTORICAL TIMELINES

Generally speaking, Chinese New Poetry is classified into four periods: 1917 to 1949, 1949 to 1976, 1976 to 1989, and 1990 to the present. A new "three-stage" conception (1919 to 1949, 1949 to 1989, and 1990s to the present) views Mao-era and Misty/Post Misty as one era.

Some of these boundary lines may be marked by political events; for instance, 1919 was the year when the May 4 Movement burst out, promoting democracy and vernacular language, among other aims. 1949 was the year that "New China" was established; 1976 was the end of the Cultural Revolution, with the death of Mao Zedong; and 1989 was the year that the Tiananmen confrontation took place in China, and soon thereafter the whole world changed with the dismantling of the Berlin Wall and collapse of the Soviet bloc regimes.

We chose 1990 as a starting point for this anthology for aesthetic reasons. In 1990, Chinese poetry began to show more innovative use of language; more narrative elements, as a means to overcome shallow romanticism; less conventional sentimentality; greater emphasis on precision in descriptions; and a notable blend of narrative and lyricism, in contrast with the predominantly high-pitched lyrical modes that prevailed in pre-Misty, Misty, and early Post-Misty periods.

The 1990s were the period in which forerunner poets such as Duo Duo and Bei Dao produced their best work, today's principle poets such as Xiao Kaiyu and Zang Di came to maturity, and younger poets such as Jiang Hao and Hu Xudong emerged. This anthology reflects the artistic vitality at least three generations of Chinese poets, including some who came to recognition in the new century.

THE SELECTION PROCESS

This project started in 2011 as part of the "Poetics of Six Continents" program, initiated and sponsored by the Harriet Monroe Poetry Institute of the Poetry Foundation. Prior to that, some of the poems were translated in 2009 as preparation for inclusion in the bilingual magazine *Poetry East West*.

The idea of an anthology arose in April 2012. The original plan was to introduce ten poets, with ten poems from each. To avoid personal biases and also to confirm my impression of the poetry scene in China, I asked twenty poets and critics in China to nominate ten to twenty poets who have made the most important and significant contributions since 1990. The "10 by 10" format was later expanded to the current scope, with newer and more familiar names assembled together. The poets are now represented by only one to ten poems, but we hope that readers will make discoveries here that compel them to look for more work by these remarkable writers.

There are twenty thousand published poets in China today, with at least one hundred especially good ones, according to the recently published thirty-volume "One Hundred Year Canon of New Poetry." It would be impossible to include in one volume all of those good poets. What we've sought to do is introduce a selection of strong work, then mention or cite other poets in the introductions, so as to present a broader picture of what's happening in Chinese poetry in the most recent twenty years. Readers will also find in the accompanying surveys the names of important earlier poets not presented in an anthology that focuses on the time period of 1990 to 2012.

Nearly half of the poets featured here are translated into English for the first time. For writers more familiar to Western readers, we've tried to choose poems not translated before, or we've presented well-known poems in a more poetic way, in an effort to bring to U.S. readers a fresh comprehension of what's going on in China today.

Chinese poetry has diversified in many directions. While some people still write in the classical style with strict formal schemes, and more experimental poets continue to write free verse, all of these writers are attempting to explore the most complex aspects of the human mind, in relation to reality. It is beyond the scope of this relatively brief compendium to represent all the trends and schools, but instead to give English-speaking readers another look at some of what is strong and thought-provoking in contemporary Chinese poetry, acknowledging that many examples have been translated and anthologized in other books. Ours will be an on-going project — to be expanded again in a few years.

TRANSLATION

The poems in this anthology have all been newly rendered into English, not previously published except in a few instances, as noted in the Acknowledgments. Among the translators are Sinologists and poets, invited to contribute in order to insure presentation of varied styles. I'm deeply thankful to all of them — without their support, this gathering would have been impossible to create.

Wen Yiduo was one of the first poets who translated Chinese New Poetry in collaboration with an English-speaking colleague. Unfortunately he didn't live to see his work published. But his effort to promote New Poetry and his approach to translation has been inspiring — interpreting the poetry as a native-speaking Chinese poet and working closely with native-speaking translators of the target language.

I have compared all the English pieces in this anthology with the original poems in Chinese, and found half of the translations to be nearly word-for-word and line-to-line accurate. The other half are "creative" translations, in various ways, but these too have retained the meanings, gestures, tones, and above all the driving forces and spirits of the originals. Effectiveness rather than superficial likeness is what we've striven for.

We take the "poet-translator" approach, as most of us are poets, including the scholar Christopher Lupke, who has written poetry earlier in his life. This approach emphasizes poetic re-creation during the process of translation, but without losing sight of the necessity for close reading of the original texts, as many of us read Chinese and/or have spent years in the study of Chinese poetry. The second part of the hyphenated approach is also important, as many of us are devoted translators, not just translating a few poems for fun.

The book's cover image of newspapers by artist Xiaoze Xie says more than I can say here in words: translators are investigators seeking to discover what's beneath the texts, in order to bring out the poetry in a way that "stays news" in another language.

Anyone translating Chinese poetry, ancient or modern, will find that the "subject" of a sentence is usually missing. The most common strategy is to assume that "subject" to be an "I" or the character in the poem. For instance, in "Mirror," the best-known poem by Zhang Zao (1962–2010), the first line tends to give translators a headache, and an easy way to render this line would be something like this: "Whenever she recalls all the regretful things in life, plum blossoms will fall." While Ezra Pound and other American poets were able to "make it new" by rendering the old Chinese formal poetry into free verse in English, what can we do as contemporaries with the New Poetry, which is already free verse? To make new something already supposedly new is a challenge. One way to deal with this problem is to break the routine strategies in translation practice. A new approach to the century-long problem of the missing "subject" is not to use a pronoun but to retain the ambiguity and multiple allusions of the Chinese original:

Mirror

Plum flowers fall whenever a regret awakes —
as in watching her swim to the other shore
or climb a pinewood ladder.
Dangerous things are beautiful;
it's better to see that she returns on horseback,
her face warm,
abashed, her head lowered, speaking back to the Emperor.
A mirror awaits her, as always,
allowing her to sit inside it, in her usual place,
and gaze out the window — regrets awaken all the plum flowers
as they fall, like egrets, over the South Hills.

镜中

只要想起一生中后悔的事
梅花便落了下来

比如看她游泳到河的另一岸

比如登上一株松木梯子

危险的事固然美丽

不如看她骑马归来

面颊温暖

羞惭。低下头，回答着皇帝

一面镜子永远等候她

让她坐到镜中常坐的地方

望着窗外，只要想起一生中后悔的事

梅花便落满了南山

(1984)

The traditional functions of Chinese language — pictographic, ideographic, sound-imitating, meaning-transferring, and so on — have always been played with in Chinese poetry as rhetorical devices. Instead of writing a long footnote about how the two key words, Plum (梅) and Regret (悔), resemble each other in shape and echo each other in sound, I used "egret" which didn't exist in the original, to demonstrate the aesthetics of this poem and how one word/conception resonates with another (regret, egret). As Zang Di may have suggested, among other insights, in his poem "Room with a Plum Tree": what the translator as an observer (and intruder) can do is to bring light to the face of beauty and let readers see, through her illuminated eyes, the mystery of poetry.

My sincere gratitude goes to the editors at Tupelo Press, especially Jim Schley, to the Harriet Monroe Poetry Institute of the Poetry Foundation, and to all of the poets and translators who have made this anthology possible.

Ming Di
Los Angeles, California

For Qu Yuan (343–278 BCE) and Wen Yiduo (1899–1946)

NEW CATHAY

新华夏集　当代中国诗选

Duo Duo

Dreamer, traveler between reality and the poetic realm, master of Chinese language, and former opera singer, Duo Duo (pen name of Li Shizheng; 1951–) fascinates readers with mysterious imagery and enchanting lines. His work blends stylized syntax with down-to-earth colloquial diction to create strange flashbacks from a tumultuous life.

Duo Duo grew up during an era when China was going through tremendous changes. He was born shortly after the 1949 change of power and a few years before Mao Zedong's 1957–58 Anti-Rightest Movement. His formal schooling was interrupted and eventually ceased in 1966 when the Cultural Revolution commenced. He was sent for "reformation" to a farm in Baiyangdian during a nationwide campaign that transferred students and intellectuals from the cities to the countryside for re-education among peasants. Remarkably, Baiyangdian became the cradle of contemporary Chinese poetry: like Duo Duo, the poets Shi Zhi, Gen Zi, Mang Ke, and others spent their youth and their early writing careers there.

In 1968 Duo Duo began writing in the tradition of classical Chinese poetry but soon found it impossible to continue in this mode and go beyond what had been achieved by ancient poets. In 1972, after encountering nine poems of Baudelaire (translated by Chen Jingrang) he immediately started writing in a completely different way. In his own words, the effect was as if "Baudelaire fired a gunshot at me."

Like other poets of his generation, and despite a lack of formal college education, Duo Duo read widely, taking or discarding what was available: Byron, Shelley, Pushkin, T. S. Eliot, Mayakovsky, Tsvetaeva, Lorca, Neruda, Plath, and so on — a truly varied combination. His literary explorations continued during his years in Europe (1989–2003), a period when he found kinship with Vallejo, Mandelstam, and other poetic exiles. Yet despite his love for Western literature, Duo Duo's poetry remains rooted in classical Chinese prosody. His work thus represents many tensions between cultures, as we see Duo Duo consciously breaking away from the massive influence of the Western tradition to carve out an approach and style of his own.

. Having gone to the Netherlands in 1989 and then remaining overseas for fifteen years, he returned to China in 2004, was warmly welcomed by the avant-garde poets, and was named Poet of the Year by the "South Daily" newspaper group. Since 2004, Duo Duo has been teaching at Hainan University in southern China; he currently divides his time between Hainan and his hometown, Beijing.

While his more recent poetry was introduced to a wider audience in 2010 when he was awarded the Neustadt Literature Prize from the University of Oklahoma and its journal *World Literature Today*, Duo Duo's earlier work has been more influential among poets in China. Part of the immediate appeal of these poems, especially Duo Duo's outpourings from the 1990s, lies in their compelling lyricism and complex use of repetition, in response to classical Chinese poetry. Readers will also find a sophisticated intentionality in this poet's unexpected, often startling imagery and metaphors. Duo Duo's body of work continues to be a unique and important part of contemporary Chinese poetry.

Unless otherwise specified, introductions to the poets
are by the editor.

Morning

it's morning or any time, it's morning
you dream of waking up, you're afraid of waking up
so you say: you're afraid of ropes, afraid of women with faces of birds, so
you dream of your father
speaking bird words, drinking bird milk
you dream of your father as a bachelor
who by chance, not in a dream
had you, you dream the dream your father dreamed
you dream your father says: this is a dream a dead man has dreamed.

you don't believe but you're inclined to believe
this is a dream, only a dream, and it's yours:
it was once the handlebar of a bicycle keeping the shape squeezed by a hand
now, it droops from your father's belly
it was once a son refusing to be born
now it's you
crawling back to that handlebar you've dreamed all the details
like the teeth your father dropped on the ground, glittering
and laughing at you
so you are not the death
but merely a case of death: you've dreamed your dream's death.

(1991)

STILL

Waking at night with snow on the forehead it's still
the same like walking on a piece of paper and it's still
like walking into the field of invisible snow, and it's still

like walking between words, wheat fields, walking
in the shoes on sale, walking to the words
The moment you can see where your home is, it's like

still standing in the empty field, fixing your suit, still
bending your knees. The gold shields. It still is.
The world's most loud, the loudest

   is, still, the earth

And the October light is passing though his legs when he's mowing, it's
like a golden corn field
with a burst of wild laughter, a burst
of firecrackers, a bright red pepper field, still, it's

the gilt that no arrangement can reproduce
the order of furious growth is a spur of October
which is persuasive, omnipresent, it's

like the cold ox dung of September shoveled in the air, it's
the stones in October walking to us, forming a team, it's
November rain passing over a place without you, still, it's

the seventy pears on the tree laughing their faces off
Your father is still the cough among your mother's
laughter

The ox moves toward our disappearance, jotting
Still it's a family sitting on the cart watching the snow
licked by a huge ox tongue

    O warm, it's still warm

And in memory, snow increases the weight of remembrance
It's what snow owes us. Snow falls to cover
the page that snow has turned over

    turned over, but still is

And the winter field understands the cemeteries
four trees planted by four trees here
the old light opens the speaking, outside words'

    cracking, but still it is

your father who saw your mother's death as the sky
and his own death as your mother's tombstone
your father's bone is walking up these hills

    and still is

the planet walks through this life
every piece of broken glass in the backyard talks
for the reason of not seeing us again, says

    still, it is still

(1993)

Watching the Sea

After the winter sea, what runs in your veins
certainly is no longer blood
You have to face the sea when you make love
certainly   you are still
waiting for the sea breezing towards you. The breeze
is certainly coming from the bed

So does memory, the illusion of the sea
remains in the dead fish's eyes
The fishermen are the retired engineers and dentists
The cotton of June the medical cotton wool
But you are still looking for trouble
in the field   certainly
The trees you walk by are knocked down, with big bumps
Their grief will certainly bring you unusual future
because you love to say 'certainly'
like the Indian women who reveal their waist

The bed where you sleep together is nearby
Certainly not far from Chinatown
And the Moon, bright like what you spit out
That, people say, is your health
What's no longer important, or what's more important, will certainly
certainly stay in your mind
like the arrogant bomb skin on the face of England

To watch the sea you must exhaust your youth
the planets in your eyes become cinders
The sea will leak from the earth to another earth

At the night that a man must die, a man dies
though the ring doesn't want to die with the body
The horse's ass with hormones in it will get excited
because sorting things means messing up
A bicycle with the chain fallen out runs faster faster
Spring wind is the green belt around the patient with kidney stones
Taxi driver's face boiled fruit
When you get home your old chair is young, certainly

(1989–90)

THE RIVER OF AMSTERDAM

November   while the night takes the city
    is only the River of Amsterdam

but look—
the oranges from my trees are on the river
swaying in the November wind
I try to close the window, it's no use
the river reverses its current, it's no use
the pearl-studded sun rises

it's no use
doves fly off like metal scraps
the street without the boys is instantly hollow inside the river

after rainfall
the roof where snails crawl
— my country
sails up to me, slowly, the waters of Amsterdam ...

(1989)

NIGHT

Tonight, symbols take us

The Moon is an anemic face circling
a mistake we call
time
Death, a doctor standing by the bed we call bed

Heartless feelings
circle
frightened feelings we call the feelings of the frightened

On my iron porch, Moonlight coughs
gently into a void
which coughs up
a suggestion of a seeable exile …

(1973)

MOVING

Winter afternoon, mice skate around
I — pretend to move out
I hammer around, taking nails out of
painting frames
and sleigh a desk to the center of the field
finding the horizon full of people
each person a handrail of a stretcher
lifting something — the flesh of the earth
quivers like gold, the trees around
all dressed like me, with a black jacket on top
the lower part — the bare trunks
read: forest for sale.

(1986)

My Uncle

I looked down from the high toilet, in my childhood
and there was my uncle, eye to eye with a bull
In their eyeball-to-eyeball
I saw one purpose:
When the light comes in, the shadows come out!

When a soccer ball flies over
the school ground
a feasible power widens my uncle's vision
to the sun
that's frozen in the high North Pole
And he wants, history, to tweeze back, into history

So I believe that the sky is the sky
that can move
and my uncle, in his frequent returns from there
is my uncle, in his own socks
which convinced me that he was going to close himself
by opening the door —
and tell his story in a flashback

He wanted to repair clocks
this old man in white socks, as if with a premonition —
to correct a
mis-saying
that had already been fixed by his time and my time:
We had all
fallen
into holes called humans!

Up to this day, the tobacco from those clouds still chokes me
I walk
along the railways in a direction of red village I call my Uncle
and see
in a wheat field my uncle's beard grows
though the man he was has long run off the earth's crust
he
and the red kerchief he stole from that village —

(1988)

The Boy Who's Catching a Wasp

No wind, no wind, only birds. Birds.
"Birds are here, but morning hasn't come."

A bird catches the voice out of a tree, and continues.
A boy enters the picture from the right.

"Little mother, all your wheat fields are coming to me."
Three suns are chasing one bird.

"Little mother, the little ox is moving in your belly."
A black horse dashes over. The blackest horse.

"Little mother, the coffin is here, from the South."
The tree looks up, measuring the boy's head.

The boy cries, and his cry stays inside a plum.
More plums and people are left outside the picture.

The boy was standing on five legs, now all his legs
become stones.

The young tree cries, unable to grow leaves.
A ripened plum joins the cry: you — us.

(1992)

Constant

They often occupy the iron chairs in the park
like the way they occupied lots of clothes
Their houses have "past lives," this city
and this world often apparate in their dreams
Their hunger isn't sated when they read newspapers
the hunger, imported from a faraway land
makes them feel they can put on more weight —
Their lives don't change but when they read news
the map expands

They were mistresses, wives, mothers,
and they still are
But no one wants to remember that
Even their pillows (where they slept with someone)
try to forget that
so they talk to themselves unceasingly,
incessantly, as if to a god
and grow kind, as if they weren't kind before

They're willing to listen now, to humans
animals, or rivers, they are ports
waiting for barks to embark
and to return
They don't necessarily want to go to Africa
they sit in their fixed iron chairs
facing homeless wanderers covered by apple tree leaves
and nod into sleep, they drowse and dream
dreaming their uteruses will be tomorrow's church

(1992)

THOSE ISLANDS

They are toes that utterly abandoned shoes
their shapes formed in their escape. By leaving
they preserve the land
like tumors in the brains, preserving time
They witness changes in the unchanging landscape
To the waves they say *No*
Their loneliness comes from the deep seabed
the fish-eaten faces of sailors
faces of those who indulge in the tormented ocean
The cries of the toothless reached there once
Loneliness is deemed to be rescue
When I arrive there with tourists like fake pearls
pouring onto the dock, I see
my shadow cast deep into the water
A plow covered with pearls
plows the deep brain into a graveyard —
Under the sand with laughter from the naval base
is a wasteland for growing words.

(1993)

王小妮

WANG XIAONI

Considered an evergreen in Chinese poetry, Wang Xiaoni (1955–) has been writing and publishing steadily from the late 1970s to the present, and she continues producing exceptional poetry when others from her generation have lost their lyrical voices after a proliferation of confessionalism in the 1980s and early 1990s. Wang Xiaoni has never been part of any circumscribed literary circle, nor has she ever carried any fashionable label; instead she has remained a quiet but visible presence, meanwhile winning numerous awards through the past three decades.

She was born in Changchun, northeast China, and after college worked as a literary editor in the film industry for a few years before settling down in the southern city of Shenzhen in 1985. She has been teaching at Hainan University for the past ten years.

With twenty-one volumes of poetry, essays, and fiction credited to her name, she is now hailed as one of the most admired female writers in the country. Critics also regard her work highly, praising her language as "crystal clear" (Tang Xiaodu) and "rustic and delicate at the same time, capturing the subtle drama in life" (Geng Zhanchun).

To the Sunlight Entering the Room

Here you are, just in time to invade my territory.
Half my desk receives your warm reach —
inventor of happiness, the tenured professor.
You come only to offer yellow heat,
leave behind ripening fruits, budding flowers,
cotton and grain bursting out — your luster
manifests in the earth's bright abundance.
But under this undergrowth there's sweat,
coughing, gasping, and blackened cracks —
don't think that I can't see this.
I refuse to be bathed in you again. Winter is trembling;
I won't accept your light.

(2010)

柏桦

BAI HUA

The poetry of Bai Hua (1956–) tends toward incongruities. His work shows many influences, above all lyricism, Symbolism, and a Romanticism in which the experiences of the individual — real or imagined — reign supreme. In most of his poems, he shows a commitment to describing tactile impressions, often set off by surprising analogies or images. He is a poet of the body's physical senses but also a poet of the philosophical mind, a breadth that gives his work a strikingly multilayered quality.

Bai Hua was born in Chongqing, and the local scenery, flavors, and dialect have never ceased to influence his work. He studied English in college and began to write and translate poetry in his twenties. After early success, publishing in prominent newspapers and journals, he stopped writing poetry altogether and turned instead to criticism and short essays. This period of poetic silence lasted through the 1990s and on into the 2000s, but in recent years he has begun composing and publishing poetry again, showing impressive vigor and a renewed conviction in his craft.

The three poems included here exemplify some of his strengths as a poet. "In the Qing Dynasty" plays with historical fact to spin out a fantasy world in which even the lanterns "understood the essentials," and the "taxes inspired the people," yet specific details fasten the poem to an actual time and place. Bai Hua often straddles this line between the absurd and the matter-of-fact, a point he emphasizes at the beginning of the poem "Reality": "This is gentleness, not the rhetoric of gentleness / this is aggravation, aggravation itself." By the end of that poem, readers are offered the ridiculous proposition that Lu Xun and Lin Yutang, two writers often on opposite sides of literary debates, might in fact be one and the same. Written more recently, "Under an Angry Wind" also has a farcical tone while maintaining an underlying seriousness about lived experience. These seeming contradictions are a hallmark of Bai Hua and make his poetry some of the most interesting to come out of contemporary China.
— *Eleanor Goodman*

In the Qing Dynasty

In the Qing dynasty
lightheartedness and idealism grew deeper
cows and sheep were idle, people played chess
the imperial examination was impartial
every place had its own currency
grain could be used to barter
for tea leaves, silk, porcelain

In the Qing dynasty
landscape painting neared perfection
paper was abundant, kites flew everywhere
lanterns understood the essentials
temple after temple faced south
the wealth seemed excessive

In the Qing dynasty
poets didn't work for a living, concerned with reputation
drinking under falling petals, in warm sunny weather
the lakes brimmed with water
two ducks swam against the wind
everything was at odds

In the Qing dynasty
one man dreamt of another
read The Grand History at night, swept at dawn
the court created a Military Office
each year selecting officials with long fingernails

In the Qing dynasty
men with and without beards

taught by example instead of with words
farmers didn't want to learn to read
the young respected the old
mothers submitted to their sons

In the Qing dynasty
taxes inspired the people
and built irrigation works, schools, temples
books were printed, gazetteers collected
the architecture was designed to look antique

In the Qing dynasty
philosophy fell like rain, science couldn't adapt
one man changed his mind night and day
always unreasonably anxious
resentment became his lifelong vocation
until his death in 1842.

(1986)

Reality

This is gentleness, not the rhetoric of gentleness
this is aggravation, aggravation itself

Ah, prospects for the future, reading, turning around
everything is slow

on long nights, the harvest doesn't come from need
on long nights, one should give up on speed

and winter perhaps is spring
and Lu Xun perhaps is Lin Yutang

(1990)

Under an Angry Wind

Was it a purple wind? What pretty thinking. It was an angry wind
the dog grew fat and barked, his ears sliced by the wind,
he wanted to eat that cupboard in your belly.

I'd just vomited collectivism from my body
gripping two inches of hot cigarette in the right side of my thick mouth
leaning on my wife's back reading, totally at ease.

So the days go by one by one …
Who says? (Fairy tales) Anderson?
It's just that that accordion has started its strange shouting again.

(2012)

张曙光

ZHANG SHUGUANG

As one of the leading poets from the 1990s and as a translator of Dante and Czeslaw Milosz, Zhang Shuguang (1956–) is well known throughout the Chinese poetry community even though he lives in a remote region, the northeast corner of the country. Born in Heilongjiang Province, he was educated and later worked there as a professor of literature. Along with Xiao Kiayu from Sichuan, he started an independent magazine in 1989 called "The Nineties," which became widely influential among poets and critics in China in the 1990s. He is now co-editor-in-chief (with Zang Di and Xiao Kaiyu) of one of the nation's most important poetry reviews.

Zhang Shuguang's poetry has an unusual musicality that's both lyrical and narrative, like the ancient folklore, with simple language but also carrying contemporary ideas. The recurrent theme of his work is snow, which has become a motif or sometimes anti-motif throughtout his writing. He sees everything as snow, and he sees snow as anything but snow. Many poets try to imitate him, but few have achieved a similar depth of thought and artistry. Many critics think that his poetry is nourished by foreign literature, but fewer have noticed that he is strongly empowered by the domestic classics.

One of the pioneer poets in introducing narrative features into Chinese poetry in the late 1980s, he became prominent nationwide as the new mode attracted many poets in the following decade. Since the beginning of the new century, his poetry has been studied and discussed across China.

Since his recent work has been widely anthologized, the two earlier poems included here are intended to show a different aspect of Zhang Shuguang's many voices and styles.

SNOW

Snow, I was surprised. The first snow
choked in my throat,
I wanted to cough, to run
from snow.
I didn't see the street, the poplars, the park benches
the conductor's whistle. Snow.
Faces of idiots abused the air
and turned to snow.
I didn't have a chance to read the "Massacre"
or "The Dead" by Joyce.
I didn't know death and snow
are colleagues.
I was three that year, Mother threw me up in the air, a tree in the yard.
Now we don't live in snow —
Mother's nostrils don't breathe. 1982.

(1986)

To Xuefei

Where is your face? flooded by what?
New York streets?
your head, tilted to one side, your neck
can't hold the weight of ideas,
where's your face? you are so clumsy
driving in Brandeis, your wife is
making souvenirs for who? a company?
and your son? in China? Why
you chose this damned
career of a poet,
I can't say …
Your father curses you, your father
I do not know, writes
in a cursive that's yours,
since you are his son and
are in America, and Allen Ginsburg
and John Ashbery
are also there and are beautiful, and you
are hot, but I don't know why
you chose this damned career as a poet.
Wind and your face, poet, is
blurry and strange, I don't understand how these lips
eat steak in a restaurant
if I see you I'll punch you and say Hey Buddy don't lick
your fingers, speak better Chinese, boy,
and I will drag you
from your wife's angry eyes to City Lights,
San Francisco,
City Lights, my Charlie Chaplin. City lights.

(1986)

孙文波

SUN WENBO

Sun Wenbo (1956–), born in Sichuan in southwest China, spent his childhood in the countryside and later went to school in the city of Chengdu. He served in the army for a few years before working in factories, and while working as a blue collar worker he published poems. He became a literary editor in the mid-1980s. Having gained recognition first in Sichuan, he became prominent nationwide in the mid-1990s when he joined his friends Zhang Shuguang and Xiao Kaiyu in editing the poetry journal "The Nineties," which promoted "narrative writing." In 1996, he was selected to be one of the few poets from China to attend the Rotterdam International Festival.

Despite his productivity, with numerous published volumes of poetry, selecting examples that show Sun Wenbo's diverse styles is difficult.

Some readers find his writing clumsy, while others consider the work to be completely transparent. There is a distinctively logical reasoning in the poems of Sun Wenbo that seems to be the basis for people blaming him for being either too wordy and too explicit. Clear or misty—these distinctions have long been a concern in criticism of Chinese poetry. If too convoluted or obscure, they'll accuse you of playing games; if too plain, they'll say you don't know the craft.

Sun Wenbo is never a simple poet. He has his own favored method and his own theory of esthetics. He rejects fragmented phrasing and disjunctive imagery in a poem: "What the heck is that bunch of 'images' doing there, saying nothing relevant?" Relevant or not is a big issue in contemporary China. Sun Wenbo is involved in many such debates, and he is trying to build a new prosody, hearkening back to that of the Song dynasty: Opening, Development, Change, and Conclusion. To Sun Wenbo, every single step is important in building a poem.

Sun Wenbo is also concerned with the relationship between individuals and society, relations between language and the world, and the relation of one thing to another in the greater order of things. He has criticized the predominant poetry of the 1970s as nonsensical, chaotic, lacking logic and theory, not poetry but slogans, because slogans don't require formation in those fundamental four steps that make up the essence of literature of any genre. As chief editor of several independent journals, Sun Wenbo has been a major influence on younger poets in China today.

BLAND LIFE, BLUNT POETRY

Apples change genes, oranges change genders,
words become absolutely tyrannical under the shadow of -ism.
I speak but say nothing; you oppose and oppose everything.
The paradox of rhetoric leads me to the way of poetry,
I travel valleys and gullies like a huge bird in the sky, only to see
fruits become symbols. Too symbolic,
the toughness of apples, the brutality of oranges. To find gentleness
I have to clear away other words from the pile. I plane off
the snobby and sneaky ones, they've been trying to use the old against ...
Or let me put it another way, they act as if they were authorities,
as if they were ministers, or even emperors, of words.
The kingdom of language is decadent. How have I tolerated it
for so long? I'd rather see chaos. I say
chaos is good! When apples fly in the air
oranges become shields against the –ism. Or when I see
apples swimming in the ocean of words like mermaids,
oranges a pack of camels carrying feelings on their backs, I feel
liberated. I feel so liberated I start writing about
the republic of apples and democracy of oranges. When I see
apples have not become tanks, oranges not bombs,
I know I've not become a slave of words after all.

(2009)

Nothing to Do with Crows

First just one, then a flock
flapping their crooked wings
before me — darkness sweeping the sky.
I watch as if watching a play unfold, a drama of nature.
A single crow is mystery, a flock of crows is fear.
Humans can't escape
the past, the consciousness — the crows
flying within me: witchcraft, prophecy, forbidden awakening.
I sit, limited: I believe what I don't understand,
trust what I don't believe, like a country
built on mistaken foundations constructing a false enemy.
I miss the days of youth, the fence of language
not yet built — only imagining, remembering —
the black crows and white snow opposite but one,
a beauty, a paradox in paradise — to vanish
was to be eternal — I watch now, the crows become fiction,
flying outside me — they're not really there, circling in old silence;
they're not really there, dwelling high on the glassy roofs.

(2006)

Poetry of Nonsense

Your snow is not mine. My snow is in the courtyard.
In early morning I walk out, find snow on the ground
with my dog's footprints — but not the way one draws
on a blank sheet of paper. No, it's a freehand landscape.
My dog draws without intention. Still I see mountains
and waters there — I see Mount Emei and River Minjiang
with clouds hanging and a beautiful woman washing clothes.
You might say I'm far-fetched, and maybe I am.
I can go even further, be more far-fetched
and say I see philosophy in the snow, not Kant
or Kierkegaard but a philosophy of fleeting moments.
Have you experienced keeping your eyes focused on something,
only to see it disappear quietly? That is happening now.
I've stood on this porch for less than an hour,
half of the ground has surfaced — things are returning
to the original form. My snow is perhaps not snow,
but something to show me the meaning of loss.

(2009)

王家新

WANG JIAXIN

Wang Jiaxin (1957–) was born in Danjiangkou, Hubei Province, and after high school he was sent to the countryside to work as a laborer. When the Cultural Revolution ended, he was admitted to Wuhan University in 1978 and after graduation worked as a teacher and editor. He went to London in 2002 as a visiting scholar and returned to China in 2004. He is currently a professor of literature at Renmin University in Beijing, and he has established the International Writing Center and International Poets Workshop there. For three decades one of the most highly regarded and widely published poets, Wang Jiaxin is frequently anthologized and is prominent as a poetry critic, editor, and translator.

Although accused in 1999 of being an "intellectual poet" during the biggest debate in contemporary Chinese poetry, other poets later criticized his work as lacking rhetorical strength. Wang Jiaxin claims that his poetry is not concerned with petty tricks and manipulations but centers itself in deep metaphor. He is best known for longer narrative poems, such as "Pasternak," "London Notes," and "Eulogy," which drew inspiration from long conversations with his literary counterparts abroad, particularly in Russia and England. After a break from poetry writing during which he devoted his time to translating Paul Celan into Chinese, Wang Jiaxin returned with a new poetic voice, more lyrical and condensed. In recent years, he has shifted his focus to capturing small moments encountered in his international travels, extending these to a metaphorical level.

Diary

He starts at the lush oak tree,
making small circles on the lawn to a larger
Circle. I listen to the gardener mowing, sniff
The grass, the freshness from the cut,
I breathe in, and enter another garden
Of my imagination where the grass is swallowing
The white marble carvings on the bench —
Waves of the grass, like death caressing me
From human fingers.

I wake up, and see an abandoned mower.
It's cold. Things around me are submitting to something colder.
The oak tree bursting out, the gardener
At rest, eternally. It starts snowing
From my pen — it will not fill the garden
But my throat. This white death, the reincarnation of seasons
Of larger death, I love
The choking white snow, the thrill of loss. I recall
The last green breath of grass...

(1992, Belgium)

Seeking the Tree

In Memory of Andrei Tarkovsky

We come to Gotland to look for a lone tree —
The tree in your last film that
Grows leaves after death

We search along the coast and find
No single tree by itself
Only woods and forests
"Impossible to survive alone"
On this windy island. A tree stands by itself
In your mind only

Even its shadow will betray it
Unless a boy waters it every day with a bucket
Taller than himself

Unless the tree grows from a seed of tears

(2010, Sweden)

OYSTER

End of a reunion. On the seaside table
Lie a few oysters
Of flower size. Unopened.

"They taste better if you can't
Open them," someone says. No one laughs
Or bothers to think what it means.

We listen to the sound of night waves and drive
Through the unending road
Of dark pines.

(2012)

廖亦武

LIAO YIWU

Liao Yiwu (1958–), born in Sichuan, became known as a poet in the 1980s throughout China, then decided to be an underground writer, deliberately. From 1990 to 1994 he was imprisoned, as a result of the long poem "Massacre." In prison he suffered terrible privations and torture but continued to write, and from a fellow prisoner he learned to play the xiao, a bamboo flute of ancient origin.

Following his release but permanently blacklisted by the government, he worked at many odd jobs to earn a living, but still he continued to write. Fifteen times his requests to leave China to attend international literary events were denied, and he fled the country in 2010. He is now a performing artist and musician, reciting his poetry throughout Europe. Author of several bestselling books of nonfiction in the United States and Germany (for instance, *The Corpse Walker, God Is Red,* and *My Witness*), he was awarded the 2011 German Geschwister-Scholl-Preis and the 2012 Peace Prize of the German Book Trade. In 2012 he became writer-in-residence at DAAD/Berlin.

One of the most powerful and original poets in China, Liao Yiwu's early writing was influenced by translations of Baudelaire, Whitman, and Ginsberg, but gradually he found his own voice, combining lyricism with narrative and elements from folk songs. He eventually abandoned the pastoral style that had earned him more than twenty awards in China and began writing dark, pessimistic, and surreal poetry. His aesthetics changed again while he was writing from prison, driven by extremity into an intense viscerality.

Of the poems selected here, the first six are from "Beauty and Death," a sequence written in 1988 for his sister Fei Fei (killed by a car) and published in 1993 in China in a Post-Misty anthology; the other four pieces are from his "Thirty Prison Poems" series, privately published in 1999 as "Gulag Love Songs," prefaced by his friend Liao Xiaobo (Nobel Peace Prize Laureate in 2010).

Rhetoric

Do not get close to these poems. Stones. Sun. Water. Do not touch.
This man-made sky. You want to control, your cowardly hands.

Each word is skin and it grows. Heals itself, the masterpiece of the
earth, the masterpiece decays before becoming the masterpiece.
Masterpiece, thin.

If you recite a line of poetry, you are tearing a piece of silk, you
are ripping off the skin. See: the wound swells, diffuses, rots idols
alive. Beauty is thin always — in paper, in snow, in feathers, silk, Wei
Li and Fei Fei, these names, thin. Control, you want. Possession,
you want. Possess nothing, idiots. Behind the decay of beauty
is emptiness, openness, loneliness. Beauty is open — dazzling,
charmingly empty.

And you, idiots, want to take control of your hands!

SEA

You want to face the sea. The sea. The sea. And not look back.

The sea of hoarse voice. The sea. Of two kissing bodies. The sea. Cut in the throat by glass. The sea. It pleads. The sea. Gasps, twists, chokes out fish from the lungs. The sea. It chokes out blood with scales, the sea. You want to live by water and fish, your vocal cord. By the sea, pray. Forget human, water. Fish, of the rubbing and squeezing and crashing of the waves, forget. Solid water and liquid fish! Forget. Then you will possess him and her, together with the woman or man of yours, or woman and man of yours. Faces and lungs. You float between two sexes. When sky understands the ocean, and turn into bright new humans, you will be among them, for sure, a member of the sky, wedded with the fish, the water, the prays of lips.

The sea, you are. Hoarse voice, you are. Not seeing us, the sea.

LEAVES

What is death? When love comes? Pleasant death. I see a soft boat. A body sleeps on the deck, leaves bids farewell to the poplars, one, two, three, and on my bald head, a leaf. "I want you" — I want you, many years ago or many years later, a human says to another: "I want you" — they are fucked up, their bodies wind-dry, like a leaf and another leaf, dropping on my bald head.

Light

Night. Flat, you lie down. You rise. Your body exposes your body to human world. Your body sees my body, takes my body, and is gone. There you are, in heaven or underground. An ocean. A roof. Human heads overturned like dregs, under the waves. Headless shells chasing the fish. Your nipples give out a flurry of sad crows. Between sky and sky. You are the candle wick of this immense water. I watch you from a distance. Light, around you, fish prowls. The headless bodies stick you on their necks. And when flood retreats? When flood retreats and earth reappears? My soul, the moment you die, are you going to recall? What? That I was the first boy you've encountered?

Snow

Outside the window is a window. Outside, is a snowfall. I sit in front of a mirror, a mirror. I am thinking of you, a mirror. A glittering inside the mirror, you. I. Cold. I feel bone cold, my bones. A girl with frozen limbs slaps me. And through my body she walks into the mirror. Is that you, the girl who has turned into a mirror?

Snow is dense, the air salty. Snow is snow, dense. From the window to the mirror, what? The snow and the mirror and the blue light. I smoke a cigarette, staying in the fluctuating puzzling cloud. Hours. Hours. Hours. And, unknowingly, hours. Unknowingly, my hair grows white.

Abyss

All dead, or they are asleep. Human bodies are so light, wax matches. Piece after piece rising and floating. I, sleepy and drowsy, stand up. My bed and cushions are gone, the street is bombarded. Disoriented, I see not an inch of asphalt underneath my feet, so I step on a floating dock built of human bodies dangling in the air. Voice. Voices. Voices. Yes, voices sing my words. I speak, also. No, I'm not singing but someone else deep in my pubic region of a throat, sings. Bits and bits of words get into my ears: ... City of Vision ... village of Sichuan ... Alafawei ... mask ... hunger ... Did I write these words? Did a hand?

Everyone is asleep on the avenue, not easy, the moment that I'm immortal. I lie down, carefully. I, clinging to the last piece of wood — it's a woman, it's a god. A god, hands clinging.

Discussing Death with Death Row Inmates

Each night of stars is a night of stars. No.
No? Each night of stars is a skull full of bullet holes.
We argue death inside brains.
We argue death under a fluorescent light
of hours.
What are hours? Shall we kneel down or stand
in the hours?
Will the bullet shoot through our chest or the back of our brains?
How is the executioner's skill? How is his aim?
Which direction will our
brains splash? the moment the soul goes out is
what?

When the body falls into a hole, with its white ass to the sun, and
the body falls into the hole
will the legs stick out, erect, high, like flagpoles?

The iron chains crash into waves of River Styx

On the eve of the shooting
doctor will pump
away 1/2 of the blood from the arm
of a man.
A man will hear the sensation of comfort
as if floating
A man's heartbeat slows down like a basketball game in the air
the dog-eating dog, larger than Saturn
barking over Saturn.

What are you waiting for, fools?
Go while it's so comfortable, boys!
You are done, earth.
The earth should sign a will and testament
of the dying people
This bastard is called God
The bastard is called God
is licking us with such a big tongue of Time

The tongue that licks the arms and legs of men
Those born from
the mouth are without emotion
And we, born from the vagina
understand what pain is.
What is pain?
Even the bad guys have mothers.

Death is a white flag
a white flag is a light
a light is in a long tunnel
What is a tunnel?
It is a lovely
train, like a penis
ejecting a bullet in climax.
It will be very uncomfortable if it misses the vital part.

It will be very uncomfortable. The anal is now speaking.
It's still a virgin.
Not fucked by the God yet.

For My Daughter

Let me sit here in this corner.
The imagined
praying cell.
With my hands handcuffed, with my hands
behind me.
Making a sign of the cross,
my hands.
For you, Miao Miao, my daughter,
a sign of the cross.

The little thing that probes and peeks,
a sign of the cross.
I eat you from the dust every day,
a sign of the cross.
The cement sunroof splits; a moon.
I see you
on that mountain, on that fog in the mountain, you in a saddle.

from READING BORGES IN PRISON

This is the most lovely hour in prison
I'm reading Jorge Luis Borges
on death row
An Argentina moon rises like a good pal
from the left face
of a Chinese prison guard
as if a knife cutting my country into two parts
Then the mountains
are what?
Sharks swim leisurely up and down
up and up,
like our bald heads one after another,
two carnations, two gunshots.

...

parachutes with no ropes

The brains in the absence
of blood.
So what?
white and red doctor and God, two gloves
taking turns
to wipe the eye balls.

Your eyes are injured by the Moon
so what?
the prison is the asphalt under your eyebrow, your bones

...

blind man, blind man
you are
betrayed, blind man
by freedom.
but you are leading us, blind man
walk to
freedom, blind man.
the prostitute that everyone sleeps with, freedom
we abandon it, afterward

the old body odor endures
on that girl.
As you have a more sensitive nose,
blind man.
Your nose,
blind man
is better than anyone's except
the police hunting dogs.

If handcuffed,
blind man
will you take your nose
as a dog, guiding you to the snow?

(excerpt from a longer poem)

To a Death Penalty Criminal

We sleep on the bed
You hold my legs on the bed
I hold your foot chains on the bed
till the stubborn iron of the bed
warms my chest.

You cover your neck with blankets
more blankets, more
blankets,
as if trying to escape from the executioner,
chopping your head with the wind.

They do it without knives nowadays!
Bullets go through
from the back
in the front chest
And pain? It will be left to your mother.
Your mother can pay the shooter
a bullet fee,
you mother can collect a corpse.

I have collected your corpse ten times by now.
Maybe you murdered
the wrong person
with your body so strong it can kill dogs.

In the name of law
this is the last inn between heaven and hell
occupied by some living dead for year long
and strangers

who are eager to get on the road
Your time is not too long, not too short.
Your body height is five feet, five inches.

You said after becoming a ghost you will go down
to the river
for a bath
and come to see me, clean.

Is that a joke? Or a will? Or the most touching
verse line
I've ever stolen from a book of poems?

My tears and my spit have drowned me in my sleep
seven or eight times
seven or eight times
but I wake up with a face as dry as asphalt
not one drop of water.
Am I a political prisoner? Why
do I always forget
my own record, why this faith
in the souls
of Tiananmen Square, and what is faith?

Faith outside the wall.
Souls outside the sky.
Year after year, old.

But this human body
is alive on earth, and
the ghost it will become is a true political prisoner.
New ghosts and old ghosts.
Political ghosts. Criminal ghosts.
Ghosts. Ghosts.

Hey you, peasant from the enormous
mountain
called China
have you ever seen tanks, boy? What is blood, boy? What is a boy, boy?

I have not seen anything other than air.
I'd rather see air. In that air
is my wife's ass, beautiful like you.

宋琳

SONG LIN

Travel is a prominent motif in the poems of Song Lin (1959–), which must be at least partly due to the poet's way of living, often on the move: from a little village in Fujian Province to Shanghai, Paris, Singapore, Buenos Aires, and back to Beijing and other cities in China. But Song Lin is not interested in travelogue; his travel is less about going to places than about a quest, an exile unbounded by place, and a search for beauty and peace in-between the familiar, already experienced world and an imagined world.

The fact that Song Lin is not always a willing traveler influences how travel figures in his work.

In 1989, he was thrown into prison for supporting the student protests; he then married a French woman and left China not knowing a word of French. In a sense he has been confined by travel, which nevertheless frees him, because the mind's eye will see realities that then need to be recorded in language. A belief in the power of imagination expressed through unexpected word combinations and imagery has been evident in Song Lin's poetics since his coming-of-age as a "campus poet" in the early 1980s. At that time, he was known for the carefree spirit and bohemian life-style that typified the "cult" of poetry among Chinese youth. Many travels later, Song Lin's emphasis on imagination is still apparent, although now more recognizably traditional Chinese themes are also reflected in his inner landscape, for instance a celebration of transcendence and abandonment, or as poet Zhang Jie has characterized Song Lin's direction — a journey of "free and easy wandering," in the truest Zhuang Zi (Chuang-Tze) sense, recalling the influential philosopher from the fourth century BCE.

Song Lin presently lives in Beijing and co-edits "Poetry Reading Quarterly." Since 1992 he has also been the poetry editor for the literary journal "Today."

—*Dian Li*

Fragments of a Letter

Forgive me for always mentioning winter and river in one breath
For talking about the cracking of ice in the air when wild geese fly by
The boat ropes in the lights, and the stars nip at the top of the Tower
People become quiet after coming into the room
They undress and go to bed, facing the wall
The last subway train crosses over the Austerlitz Viaduct
And enters District 13
The face of a drunk flashes from coal cinders in sweet sleep
A man walks in the gigantic night of the city and passes through
The dancing snow and the heavy perfumes of a prostitute

(1998, Paris)

WRITING OBSESSION

It's true: sometimes this is what he is:
Experiencing euphoria with a crazy speed
And burying himself in time. Under night's

Caterpillar tracks, he imagines a skull's sickle
Cutting down bundles of useless words —
By accident, he picks up a metaphor

As carefully as a photographer works in a darkroom
He works until dawn. His face unconstrained
As the negative of everyday living

A portion of a dim memory brings up
The brightness of the day and the darkness of the night
Distant childhood is developed from old age.

Here, a speck gradually takes shape
The dilating parts look like a soul
When it gets blown up
A mosquito's cry might give out more decibels.

Desire is motivation; style is hygiene
Pretext, suggestion, adding or subtracting meanings
Naming is intemperate, and a lie has no opposite

Sometimes this angle is the right angle
Like a line read aloud in the past tense
Once again, death rinses him

(1997)

A Cat at the End of the Experiential World

A masochistic cat is more at ease than you
while you sleep, soft paws stepping over your body.
The iron-barred window, a perfect two-way path.
This cat isn't the cat
I'm talking about now,
nor any imagined, scruffy cat.
It washes its face in a strange fashion.
Its tail shoots up; its shadow falls over the river.
When raining, its hopes mildew in the corner.
However deep your sleep,
your brain will detect the patter of its paws.
Excited, it whaps the newspaper from your hands,
spilling a bottle of milk on the table.
Its eyes glare at you with impatience and animosity.
When you awake, it still hovers near,
weird, cold, moustache spearing the air.
At the end of the experiential world
it cuddles up wearily, like a postman stranded
in magnificent snow.
And so you wait in vain. I believe
this sort of cat treats itself worse than it treats you.

(1986)

萧开愚

XIAO KAIYU

Xiao Kaiyu (1960–) was born in the village of Heping, Zhongjiang County, in Sichuan Province. In his youth he was interested in literature and culture, and he studied Chinese medicine in college, graduating with a degree in 1979. After several years of practicing traditional medicine in Sichuan, writing poetry on the side, he moved to Shanghai in 1993 where he worked as an editor, taught in a university, and began publishing his poems. In the late 1990s, he spent three years in Germany, learning the language and reading widely in European literatures. After returning to China, he eventually took up a position as professor of Chinese at Hunan University in Kaifeng, where he works now.

Xiao Kaiyu is among the poets often referred to in China as "intellectual" or "academic." And yet rather than evincing an ethos removed from everyday life, the "new intellectualism" of Xiao Kaiyu's poetry exhibits linguistic density, a layered structure of literary and cultural allusions, and extended control of subject matter. Some of his most distinctive works, such as the long poem "Homage to Du Fu," are lengthy meditations on contemporary life in China, imbued with a consciousness of the nation's history. In the past fifteen years, Xiao Kaiyu's writing has become more experimental in syntax and diction, and he now appears to be interested in pressing language to its referential boundaries.

There are few poets in China today who subject their work to the degree of revision and polishing characteristic of Xiao Kaiyu. Although little known in English-speaking countries at this point, Xiao Kaiyu's poetic seriousness will work in his favor, and surely he will eventually be seen in the West as a poet of great maturity and inventiveness. His poems, though modern and stylistically avant-garde, exhibit an awareness of China's rich past, for Xiao Kaiyu's training in traditional medicine included rigorous instruction in Chinese culture, philosophy, and literature as well. While deeply committed to his ongoing meditations on contemporary China in the midst of dealing with the Maoist legacy and the impact of increasingly more robust capitalism, in his poems he always views these issues with a sensitivity to the historical sources of Chinese culture.

— *Christopher Lupke*

WRITTEN FOR A PHOTO OF THE DECEASED

Your Roamer watch is no longer moving for you
But it's not running any slower for us,
Tonight what I saw and heard surpasses
What the tips of your feet endured at the parties
In Old Shanghai. The mood of the stock market, pornographic
Novels on the web, the dark strength in various places,
... Are even more boisterous than you yearned for.
You should remain in this chilly, little room,
Drinking tea, wrestling with a ghost, this
Is your time,
You are even more unfortunate
Than your times, getting a share of the minute shards of hostility.

You and Your connection with the world
Is only a photo of the deceased, from the frigidity in your eyes
One can see the fraudulence of fate,
You scrutinize a chest badge, like you're pondering
An idol who lost its powers. Between the idols you've overturned
And the new ones you've created there is a sea of significance,
Did you really believe animals and plants were instigated by inspiration
(or God)?
Democracy,
The contradictory apparatus you worshipped,
You use the impetuousness
Of confronting a tiger to appease the conflicts of their internal needs.

Your Roamer watch is no longer
Moving for you, I, the one you spit on, am studying
The aphorisms, the truth, and the tiny Chinese greens.
Your hopes and desires are exactly what I loathe,

Or from inertia to enjoy the quietude of interchange.
If I could, I wouldn't go to your house either
And replace you at the side of your faithful wife,
Her happiness is precisely our flaw,
We published *The Complete Works of Freud.*
Though you're good at it, you wouldn't want to come to this
Flying but not soaring world, in the window
You've accomplished what you set out to accomplish.

(1995)

THE GARBAGE EATER

I rushed toward the street in the stifling heat
And entered a small lane,
A breeze hit me as I turned in,
And at the corner, there he was, bent in the breeze

Eating garbage intently.
His long hair was clumped together like a blue garbage can,
His tongue nimbly
Curled over a bottle cap.

He was completely naked
Filth donned him in a black speckled long gown,
From head to toe,
From beginning to end as I remembered him.

At the end of 1968, one night
He crossed over the southern hills in the pitch black
Not yet to my house, he said:
"I can't walk any more."

Ah, he's a worn-out soldier!
In the midst of the battle that just ceased,
He captured the low peak of Taiyang Mountain,
From a temporary broadcast station on the summit he sang out
        a passionate victory song.

Why did he flee over night?
Why not bask in the ecstasy of his base?
Why run faster than the bird flies?
Why sleep so soundly?

He happily etched death
Upon his body,
Coming from another province,
Maybe, coming from another world,

His tongue stuck out slightly
From a pallid sliver in his lips, as if delivering
Some news but not
His corpse suddenly

Prostrate on the floor, cheekbones protuberant
In the pitch black of the night he was buried
In the dark earth.
A cavern of dark memory.

What was his name?
What use was a name (or anything else) to him?
A head stretched out from the garbage can
The bright colors there for him to enjoy.

He arose from amid the garbage,
And saw me, then immediately
Buried his head back down
Licking a fissure in a can.

Is he an angel? An angel
Visiting this reality? Or is he
Taking leave of garbage and the garbage eaters
And going, going deep into a small lane.

(1991)

THE PEOPLE'S BANK

The cluster of buildings in Shanghai's business district —
    "Lu's Mouth"
Was drooping its priceless cranium in the gray mist of evening.
In the main rectangular lobby of the People's Bank
Guards with pockmarked faces were stationed to keep out people
    like us.
We are not bankers or relatives of bankers.
We are not the people the bank is scheming against.
We are the people, men and women.
Totally perplexed and utterly joyous.

The mothers of the bank sit straight and vigilant,
Old but powerful, their tongues mulling numbers.
The numbers are alarming,
Most have the acrid taste of bitterroot in their mouths.
A few are flying high on a cocaine buzz.
A majority come from multiplication,
Piling things in a savage and empty manner
Toward the diarrhea of a one-time freedom.

Those who fear the multitude of people
Register at the lectern, and slink out of the meeting area to
    the bank.
I announce that I am a proletarian poet,
Yet I adore leisurely walking the Bund and Lu's Mouth.
The enigma is like high-voltage electricity coursing through
    a chair
Vanquishing the network of nerves, The riddle is
    In deep silence.
Fewer than people but still greater than people.

(1997)

Mao Zedong

By cutting off excessive colors and shapes
the Great Man makes the content clear.
He prefers the silver of clouds — the azure blue
of the sea — the grandeur of things
in tidy appearance. He loves this kind of a country.

The sun is fixed like a badge on the forehead
above an ocean of people.
Forged in steel, a vast reality
weaves the infinite into a finite but illusive square
built around the tower, made not of purpled gold but clay.

Newspapers cheer the ideal victory,
the unruly tide rises.
A hurricane of a hundred million hearts lifts the drooping banners
and sweeping waves sail the seawater to a new height.
The sea has only wrecks and submarines.

He lies in his study, once a swimming pool
now filled with ancient books, and stares into the air,
speaking short cryptic phrases, in a thorny voice, riddled
with indecipherable meanings, a soldier's language
from an unseen battlefield, who can understand him?

(1987)

THE STORY OF A BOATMAN PERUSING
JACK LONDON'S FICTION

Circumnavigating a submerged reef, my fleet was tossed
In the crashing waves,
The fleet advancing straight forward
Plowed through the sea —

Thrilled, I spied the sea deep: "Welcome!"
Shouted the unfathomable watery realm,
Bluer than blue and rippling into the expanse,
And group calisthenics of fish forming words.

Over and over I called out in warning, "windstorm" in the ocean
                of the mind.
And I beseeched the petrels flying overhead
Lift our team in your bills.
I was brimming with tears, mutely.

(1992)

In the Park

Today, my wish has been granted, at four in the afternoon,
Reclining on a long bench in Sun Yatsen Park, I slept like
I'd renounced the world. Awakening, I thought I'd lost everything.

It wasn't from a woman practicing Mulan boxing
Or the kids kicking a ball, but rather a lost moment
As I sat on the edge of the lawn,

Something was concealed. The belly of a pregnant woman
And the buzzing of an airplane flying in the sky over the park.
More and more of a break.

Once I thought that the sky was a bank
That would lose all its assets, a storm and an empty cave.
I, have nothing to provide for the loss.

What I've had doesn't belong to me when I see it,
When I'm talking it's already disintegrated
And lost all its value.

I know that the attire of tear-stained relatives from the disheveled funeral
Is not the breath of the dead,

                              Or humility. Oh, not that.

(1997)

吕德安

LÜ DE'AN

Lü De'an (1960–) was born in a small town in Fujian, along China's southeastern coast. He quit high school and later went to an art school to learn painting. He lived in New York City from 1991 to 1994, working as an artist, and then returned to China in 1995 to build a cabin in the mountain area of his hometown, where he has continued to write and paint.

He has been a highly acclaimed poet in China since the 1980s but has kept a low profile for almost three decades and avoided debates and controversies. He was published alongside Yu Jian and Han Dong in their unofficial but influential magazine "Them" in the 1980s and 1990s, and while the other two have since become famous, Lü De'an largely escaped notice until his third collection of poetry came out in 2011, when "Time Magazine" in China hailed him as a homegrown Robert Frost.

Poets and critics have consistently praised Lü De'an for his solid craftsmanship. As Yu Jian (1954–) has written, "We finally have a few real poets who stand independently like big trees with poetry texts as heavy as stones, showing distinctive personalities. And here I'm referring to Lü De'an."

Lü De'an still lives quietly in his self-built cabin in the mountains of Fujian, and he continues to travel between there and New York. He has never been known as an "exile" poet in the United States, but he has chronicled his experiences as a truly marginalized artist living somewhere "between" two countries and two cultures.

The poem "Offenders" is about migration, and he compares people with stones that rolled to another country after the "decisive moment" in 1989. Those who stayed inside China have become "forbidden cities of souls," while those who fled or were expelled are "firmly convicted." As to the occurrences of 1989, "what was hoped for has not been hatched." And yet this poem can be referring to any situation in human life, for the poet doesn't criticize what happened in 1989 directly but expresses a certain hopelessness, the belief that there is no escape in any country. Those who stay are ruined. Those who leave are considered dirt; but whom have they offended, and how did they become trash? He is not searching for answers but just painting the situations, the atmosphere, the feeling. He is not looking for empathy, either. In his poems, he paints layers and layers until the dried paints crack, a door opens...

OFFENDERS

I've seen the secret migration of stones.
They roll down from above, vigorously,
some of them disappear completely,
others stay but become ruins.
Nothing can be more embarrassing than
being a stone that stays behind, a towering pile,
a long shadow. I've seen them in daytime
scattering in the courtyard, a bunch of no surprises
when you walk out of the gate, but at nighttime
they scare you with their black whirring. In fact, it's only
an illusion: one piece suppresses another,
as if in an instant the whole pressure will crush your body.
Like in the beginning, someone was expelled
out of there, and there a gate was established,
and Heaven erected. Oh the labor-ridden stones,
the oval eggs, but what was hoped for
has not been hatched.
We only hear the sound at first, then we see
the stones moving, moving into our perspective.
We know it's the movement of the land,
the loosening of the earth, and the beginning of rolling.
They scramble vigorously, making you feel empty.
Yes, it's the decisive moment.
We happened to pass by at that time, not knowing
where to place ourselves. Like the stones,
some of us stayed, others continued to move forward.
Those who stayed behind became forbidden cities of souls,
and those who disappeared were firmly convicted …

(1995)

STREET MUSIC

They park their black jeep on the curb
and leave the music on
to blare on its own
into the street.

They gather around it
to keep the beat
but mostly they drift away
and let the music run
on its own.

The street is drifting up
above the city
away from other streets
like an emptied nest
blown free from the branches of a tree.

All night long
the music holds the drifting bodies together —
their shadows gather and disperse
on and above.

The homeless on the roadside
join them, swaying their light bodies
in their empty dreams.

(1992, New York)

MY GIRL

She grew up with me, my next-door neighbor
born in the season of flowers but
stricken with polio.
I walk and jump and run.
She shifts her walker along to reach the door,
while I cross the barrier with a simple lift of one leg.

The shadowy wings in her eyes scan the floor,
a sun in her room sings
but indifferently. She sits low,
a fairy with withered legs
that keep shrinking as she grows

and grows into a woman, to find the pain
the moment I raise my legs
and walk away.

She'll get used to
being stuck to the ground forever,
restrained step by step
until the shadowy wings in her eyes take her
to where I run and disappear.

(1985)

The View

Years of watching and seeing nothing,
I finally move the window away.
Or it's actually the frame
that I've removed. The window remains —
in the dark hole, the world remains.
But after all I've left there.
I've walked away from it, far away,
but still, bearing the frame on my back,
and looking through, I see myself
among the migrating birds over the horizon
repeatedly flying from one place to another,
saddled with the past.

(1989)

WHALE

On a winter's night, a pod of whales made their way to the village,
taking possession of half of the land, quietly,
like the mountains at our doorsteps. They wouldn't leave
No matter how hard we tried to persuade them. What's to be done?
Dark, stubborn, unresponsive. So we simply shouted
into the deep holes of their mouths.
But what we heard was mostly our own voices.
We tried to light their eyes with lamps: a forbidden sea.
We tried to weigh their mysterious weight,
the strength gone, becoming nothing, endless nothingness.
What's to be done? They just wouldn't leave.
They just wanted to live with us.
They wouldn't even allow us to bring the morning tide
before breakfast.
These creatures, as huge as God
blocked our way, delaying time.
When we opened the window, the sea was a few yards away.
But in their eyes, we could see they didn't welcome it —
they created a historic suicide.
Died. Their death and their weight
oppressed the land for a long time
like the mountains at our doorsteps. People brought their tools,
descended ladders, determined to take the fat
and make it into lamp oil for the church.
The rest would go to the families. Then like digging holes,
one hole led to another, each moving in its own direction.
As if digging in the earth, but the more you dig the more earth.
If you hit stones (questionable bones), just

remove them and build them into walls — so they will become
faded, become history, become ruins — alas,
everywhere, everywhere would smell of fish
and the minty truth, even today,
they are still compelling,
unlike the whales — they suddenly appeared like night,
distrustful, and depressing.

(1992)

Tempus Fugit

The sickles cut like lightning,
the grass retreats, not far away a bird
escapes, startled into the air.

You snatch an egg from the grass
before I can call out — blades part to one side,
light floods in — almost transparent.

And now we drink and laugh about that moment:
the way you bent over as you pocketed the egg
without hesitation, and how from behind

your butt seemed to apologize to the bird flying away.

(1995)

冯晏

FENG YAN

In recent years Feng Yan (1960–) seems to have emerged from nowhere, already a mature poet in age and in artistry; previously, her name had never appeared in articles or anthologies outside China, although she has been publishing poetry continuously since the early 1980s and she has been associated with a small circle of fine poets in northeastern China.

Born in Inner Mongolia and raised in Wuhan City of central China, she later moved to Harbin in the northeast. She missed the opportunity for a college education because of moving frequently, yet she has read more than most poets in China.

She is known as "a poet of mind," a judgment that mixes praise and criticism, implying that she stays away from personal emotions. In 2010 she won the Su Manshu Poetry Award along with Wang Jiaxin and Zang Di (both included in this anthology), and from that point Feng Yan's reputation has grown considerably. She has a very unique style, different from the so-called "female writing" prevalent in China since the 1980s, which resulted from the influence of American confessional poetry in translation. A line in one of Feng Yan's poems describes her well: "Like a vulture, I fly with force, calm, and precision."

from CYCLE

When new flowers are born
but continue to use their mother's names, you
see it as Spring and the old bodies of earth
exude a rich aroma
so next time you smell your grandmother think of new blessings
and how dusts
wake up
their tiny rosy cheeks.
And, sun, in surprise, sun emits
scraps of glass that escaped from the captivity
of history
and now flash out light, light, light, which is our old experience.

That is when injured seeds grow new cells from stone cracks,
and what are flowers to do but wave in the wind
like good party members,
whose feelings and promises repeat themselves
in the sunlight, and our love,
when it's awakened with new excitement
on this guarded land, is far away.
...

(2002; *excerpt from a longer poem*)

REVERSE

Anxiety and time. Destroys it even if you retrieve the time.
Run!

You rebel, you push yourself back
to the beginning, all possible paths open.
But under the dim light, you can't see the pain.
You can't hear the cries.
Rainy night. Chaos.
Anxiety is a luxury. I comb my hair —
the running ants become curious about my life.
Chaos.
The cries inside me, like sharp weapons,
stab repeatedly.

I try to retrieve the lost time, and let the shadow under the sun
fly up like silk.
I run.
I put down grace.
I put down love, silver scenery.
I run before Sartre, make existence worthless.
I run out of Wittgenstein, I move backward against his spin.
Like a vultures, I fly with force, calm, and precision.

But when I stop, time goes back by itself—
on the red bricks I hear the sound of a wheelchair rolling:
my father is walking toward me …

(2012)

杨小滨

YANG XIAOBIN

Born in Shanghai, Yang Xiaobin (1963–) graduated from Fudan University in 1985 and worked at Shanghai Academy of Social Sciences until 1989, when he moved to the United States to study. He obtained a PhD from Yale University in 1996, subsequently taught at University of Mississippi until 2006, and is now a Research Fellow at the Institute of Chinese Literature and Philosophy, Academia Sinica, in Taiwan.

While he is an accomplished scholar of modern literature with seven published books of criticism, he has never given up the writing of poems, a dedication that in his case goes hand in hand with research and critical work. He has published three poetry collections and has won several awards, including a first-book award in 1994. He has served as guest editor of "Modern Poetry Quarterly" (Taiwan) and has been actively engaged in poetry activities in mainland China, too. His poetry is distinguished by its unusual use of syntax and its mixture of seriousness and playfulness.

Yang Xiaobin is one of the pioneers of a poetry aesthetic that promotes innovations in language and an "optimistic" outlook. He sings his sorrows with a joyful tone, and he criticizes corruptions with cheerful gestures.

The Clay Pot in Tennessee

I brought a Chinese clay pot to Tennessee,
smashed it, and the aroma of fish soup bloomed,
lifting and wafting like flower petals in the spring air
before settling onto the muddy pond of a grocery store.

All the catfish grinned. So happy, they almost devoted
themselves to the broken pieces — with another pot of noodle soup
their kisses still would only reach the lady-boss's rosy cheeks
with a seal of the Overseas Chinese Association.

An unpatriotic clay pot cannot grow into a mushroom cloud,
nor has the time to nurture a nation's fine taste through small talk.
I lie down in Tennessee, kneading the fish lips that are licking the clay,
as if only through breaking can a pot's fragrance become strong.

(2005)

臧棣

ZANG DI

Zang Di (pen name for Zang Li; 1964– ,) was born in Beijing and started writing poetry in the early 1980s, then became well known in the 1990s for his sensitivity, resistence to sentimentality, originality in imagery, and unconventional use of language.

He is one of contemporary China's most creative poets, despite a thoroughly academic background: he obtained BA, MA, and PhD degrees from Beijing University and has been teaching Chinese literature there since 1996. He is an influential poet-critic and chief editor of "Chinese Poetry Review." His essays on the rising generation of poets have identified and promoted new voices in the Post-Misty age, and his book-length essay criticizing Bei Dao has been among the most controversial topics in current Chinese poetry studies.

Author of eight collections of original poetry, Zang Di has earned acclaim throughout China for producing some of the country's most exciting new work.

Neil Aitken, Canadian poet and co-translator of Zang Di, has noted that "Zang Di's poetry reflects a rich and complex interweaving of ideas and influences, engaging both Chinese and Western literary and cultural traditions. Often described as avant-garde, his poems in many respects do indeed blaze a trail well in advance of other contemporary Chinese poets, rejecting conventional sentimentality and overt social commentary, and choosing instead a more postmodern and experimental approach...His poems defy easy definition and interpretation, exploring instead the slipperiness of language through wordplay and association. There is always humor and wit, and a provocative mind at work behind each poem. One is struck by the constant interplay...between existentialism and postmodernism, abstraction and concrete detail, innovation and tradition. His poems draw on the work of Wallace Stevens, Rilke, Paul Klee, Sartre, Nietzsche, and Marquez, among many others — in dialogue or in counterpoint, Zang Di's poems participate in an ongoing symphony of ideas."

Many of the strongest poets in China today have been influenced by Zang Di one way or another — by his poems and critical essays, the poetry he has edited and translated, and the poetry series he has curated, which has featured emerging poets as well as luminaries. He has received numerous national literary awards in China, yet he is still hardly known outside the country.

JAMES BALDWIN IS DEAD

It snowed very little — a sign of loneliness
that lasted many years, quietly,
like a mysterious contempt

When a heavy snow bursts
death will have to be offered
as a body that contradicts it

and constitutes a great obstacle.
What death desires most
is the body that it had to endure

James Baldwin's body
is qualified, in the background of snow
He looks more impressive than death

A luxurious victim
he turned pitch-black in the snow
and so did the snow in his spirit

(1987)

Contemporary Love

At this moment, what I must say
bores me to death. Let me
close my eyes to dream about an ant
carrying the seed of a corpse in search of the legendary sower
A woman can finish in one night
telling her whole life story of love
and God has to forgive her

She claims to know true love more or less
and tells me: "I'm yours"
But looks as if she's declaring
"I could be yours," or
as a reward: "You are mine too"
She loves so miserably that
she can't wait to take off her clothes

As usual, she appears in a hurry
even takes off one of her breasts
that was pressed under her Wacoal blouse
which remains an exquisite gift
that seems to confess something reasonable
Indeed she loves miserably, her nude body
red from top to bottom, like a welt from Nietzsche

(1988)

In Memory of Wittgenstein

After a person dies, birds continue to fly.
This is the scene I watch.
When the scene disappears, the birds are still flying.
I'm concerned about these types of things.

Wittgenstein is a bird.
He wasn't, but he is now.
Before, people had many choices after death.
But few people are inclined to become birds.

Of course, I can explain it this way —
I was a bird before, but now
I am a person watching birds fly over his head.
Flying is so pure, like the free fall of snow.

I continue to watch,
as Wittgenstein continued to be brilliant
in the name of a bird. What a wonderful space
as if the space had died once.

(1994)

The Universe Is Flat

The news came on the radio
when I was in the kitchen
slicing cucumbers. Two cucumbers,
skin scraped off,
and cut into round flat pieces —
This is just one outcome.
To soak the slices in the small world
of sesame oil, salt, and rice vinegar,
is to be tied to another outcome —
How many people are coming to dinner?
Any unexpected guests?
How many real ingredients will conflict?!
Or, equally related to the outcome,
why does it make me happy
to hear someone announce on primetime
that the universe is flat?
Wonderful! Or, is it really that wonderful?
My intuition might not be accurate,
but it's strong like the tides of light,
the same way as when I look around the kitchen
for a brief moment —
the chopping board is flat, the knife is flat,
and all the lids, large or small,
are flat. Only the plates are not just flat
but vividly patterned.
The masks, true or false, are flat;
the pills are flat, and when
the most beautiful woman lies down
even the gods are flat.

(2002, California)

A FEW REASONS WHY I LOVE RIMBAUD

His name carries blue waves,   .
a strange love-hate
that doesn't hurt. Slow waves that rise and fall —
like a spectroscopic phenomenon.
At least, I'm fond of this odd way
he was introduced to us.
Destined to be born in southern France,
then to go to Paris, to Brussels,
to London, to wild Africa
to find enough sand.
People wash things with water, but he
washed things with vast quantities of sand.
I understand all this, and love
the glittering part of it.
I can't be sure though, if I would take him
as a poetry brother had I been born
a hundred years earlier. But I know
I like him, because he said
everyone was an artist.
His reasoning was very straightforward:
being a genius himself, he saw genius
in everyone, either potential,
or unknown. His appeal,
simple but complex. "Quoi? — L'Éternité."
It's funny that when I sleep at night,
I occasionally think he was talking nonsense,
but when I wake up in the morning, bathed
in the freshness of early light, I realize
he was certainly foresighted.

(2002)

Association of How to Conditionally Grasp the Truth

The little thing that we call "snow,"
what would dogs call it?
How does a dog tell the color of snow?
I mean, in the dark
we can't see anything, but a dog
can see his surroundings clearly,
even the hidden things.
In the dark, dogs can see further than us.
Fortunately, this doesn't involve
instincts that they have but we don't.
Dogs like to bark
at the shadows moving in the dark.
But at the drifting snow
they never make the slightest sound.
Dogs adapt their alertness to various situations,
including the quietness of morning snow.
When I walk my friend's dog,
I notice that he likes the footprints in the snow,
he pees into them — with the same expression
as when he watches me add water
to the dough that's almost ready.

(2005)

THE BOOKS OF HUMAN-SHAPED BAKERIES

I pick it up, to my surprise,
life can look as strange as a small paper bag.
But it can't be just a paper bag —
it's my home, hanging in the air,
or, just being tied up. It's also
a small bakery hotel, a little crowded,
but the best distance will soon emerge.
I invite people to make me, because I never trust
exchange in other forms. What I like most
is to invite strangers to eat me. In this way
I can travel to a strange place.
I like to visit people's hearts, across the belly.
This performing is indeed an ancient art.
Also ancient is the artistic way I was brought back
to the surface of life. People knead me,
create me, bake me, help me grow mature —
as if the joy of creation can be shared.

(2006, Tokyo)

In Memory of Paul Klee, A Book Series

Through sin I met you. A woman of full lines,
you painted her. Perhaps this was an opportunity
to relearn the world. A woman that
could solve all problems. At least, you've imagined so.
Perhaps you've dealt with this kind of inspiration,
and decided to have her undress and lie down on tree branches
where in the past, she'd only used a sofa or bed.
You did what a great artist can do —
change the background, change one's future.
I was sixteen that year, neglected my math studies
because of *The Scarlet Letter;* and because of *Wuthering Heights,*
I discovered that the self can be reformed;
because of *Sense and Sensibility,* I fell into daydreams;
I found that empathy meant to fly-flap the *Confessions.*
If there's a truth, and if you really want to understand,
then it was the great temptations that enriched me. It was
the first time I realized my body wasn't completely mine.
I resisted, knowing my body is often not in my flesh.
Three or four meters away, my body becomes
a date tree. There are two trees in the yard,
one is a date tree, and the other is a date tree as well.
This is no nonsense, but an exercise in rhythm
concerned with where you really want to position the world.
Even now, temptation still enriches me.
You see, my situation and theirs are not the same.
Every eight years I will want to quote you one more time —
How I want to humbly kneel down, but to whom?

(2009)

The Books of the Original Role

Years ago my body missed me.
This shouldn't have happened, but in fact,
did, many times. My body is my miracle,
which sounds presumptuous, but what I was thinking
was how miracles constrain my freedom, and even
constitute another form of corruption. My body hanging there,
like a ripe apple that could fall at any time.
You know, if it strikes you on your head by chance
the world will probably crack open, awakening.
I lie on my side on the grass, surrounded by the thoughts
of summer insects. I like things with a rhythm.
On the grass, the insects thought rhythmically without tuning.
Following that rhythm, it seemed as if I'd seized
fate by its Achilles' heel.
I'd brought a half-bottle of wine, the beef jerky I was chewing
full of the yak's life. I was grinding down my own body
that would not miss me anymore. My body
was once the three yaks who had just emerged from the valley.
There, the snow-streams on the Aba were like clear strings
that had melted the memory of hard granite stones.
My body missed me, meaning that from the beginning
my body was a composition of bodies
from a man and the one who returns from death.
They've brought me joys that contradicted each other like the truth.
However, what is blind is never the body itself.
You know, I could have explained this much better.

(2010)

In Memory of Dostoevsky, A Book Series

She walked into her opposite: a small life
in a big city. Shrimp aren't fresh; chives, soaked for two hours,
still smell of chemicals. In the world of men, there's no ideal man.
Once realistic, good men are more complicated than just being good.

Nothing seems to stop her.
Not just now, but nothing from the beginning.
For you, a cup of tea and a piece of cake can make you stop.
A small dish of pine nuts would be even better.

However, you are actually sharper than her — she doesn't realize it.
You hold a poetry hammer in your hand, and she moves
at the same speed that nails are being tapped.
She wants to prove there is more than one logic.

Something unprovable makes her manic in love.
It seems to be a trap from the start. She thought she was a trap
herself, deeper than poetry. She waits to be pulled like a nail
from the iron board of life. You have a hammer, but would you dare?

(2010)

哑石

Ya Shi

Ya Shi (pen name of Chen Xiaoping; 1966–) has an alchemical genius — in his poetry we are confronted by thoughts and experiences that should not, strictly speaking, be possible. Language, the body, and contemporary Chinese life are all transformed, transmuted into something that feels living and natural and yet simultaneously thrills us with its tendency to ignore the ritual strictures that make our world feel safe. The critic Yi Hang describes his work as "combining the ability to understand complexity, the power to perceive in new and fresh ways, and a bizarre imagination." He goes on to note that "Ya Shi's poems also have a sorcerous, inhuman, fantastic quality, even though his subject matter is real experience from contemporary culture…" In Ya Shi's poetry, we experience more than beauty, drama, fear and comedy; we see the way in which the work of lyric can turn the raw material of ordinary life into an incantation, a talisman.

Ya Shi was born in the city of Guang'an in Sichuan province and raised in a small village. His poetic sensibility was deeply influenced by his upbringing: his work reflects the lushness of the mountain forests, the richness of folk legend, and the macabre spark of ancient ghost stories. In the early 1980s, he won the opportunity to study at Beijing University, and now teaches mathematics at a university in Chengdu. In 1990 he turned to poetry, publishing three full-length collections and serving as an editor of the path-breaking avant-garde magazines "Subway" and "Poetry Mirror." His poetry has won several awards including Liu Li'an Prize.

With the exception of "Cryptic Poem," the following are from Ya Shi's celebrated 2007 book "Qingcheng Poems." "Cryptic Poem" was written in 2009 and collected under the title "Carved Insects" — a self-effacing reference to poetry as a minor and inconsequential art, a kind of painstaking handicraft. The title also serves as a reminder that the careful craft of these poems is exactly what

produces their feeling of spontaneity and wild magic: the eldritch moment when inanimate art shakes the dust off its wings and begins to breathe.
— *Nick Admussen*

Cryptic Poem

The bang bang of literature's slavish heart and the bruising after,
you bang bang bang, I bruise for no reason at all.

A stand-up guy, perched on the excavator, extends its metal arms
and the moment of exposure, of shame

condensed into a twinkling, lasts almost forever!
The summer dew writes back, says you're still not cryptic enough.

Fury has many categories: flattering, hair pinned in tight bun,
stream of cat piss, unaggrieved, engrossed by the broken soul …

Does the glittering system abet weakness?
The fish bone chorus is violent, cracking the scenery but blocked
          in the throat.

What's most serious doubtlessly happened before all the talking.
Swashbuckling heroism? Haven't seen it in ages. On heaven and
          earth's

temporary chopping block, you can put fir, white oak, red pine …
Spirit and the flesh, sliced until they're so lean!

(2009)

Graveyard · Scrub Forest

Probably a mile from the stone house in a ravine
there's a graveyard so battered it's hard to pick out
a few coarse bits of scattered sandstone from another angle
though appears a meticulous secret pattern
especially after rain when there hangs a limpid, persistent
idea that when entering the dense scrub forest to the left
there will be an insignificant, richly magnetic sound
arriving from the right to dissolve in the body's softest parts.
I believe all this has been carefully considered
including my arrival including this half-circular scrub forest
which has maybe just bubbled up here, impossible to fully describe
here the limbs of some members have already gone ancient and black
some others are shaken by light dripped down onto their heads
those leaves just like the skin of babies, blue-green, translucent

(1997)

Eyes of Small Animals

Honestly with regards to the creatures of the valley
I feel ashamed can't look them in the eye
inside which is violet fog (pulled along, rustling)
and kindness, placed into the eternal interrogation that is
cowardice. When the twilight follows me back to the stone house
they emerge from their many secret places
create me and wait for this wrinkled, moist,
tree-barked man to be supplanted by a steadier messenger.
Even if I hide myself in books, which open to me conveniently
I know they'll still peek out from the white spaces in words
watch me and mutter about the humiliations they'll suffer, the dirt.
Yeah when my teeth loosen and drop out one by one from age
I will still remember all of this steadfastly
and with my soul I'll answer the endless accumulation of innocence

(1997)

Measure

Noon sitting beneath the treetops where the great pines
open wide their robes like an earthen jar, shaken but silent.
I confirm that the strength alien to all people
slowly nears me: if the webs between the branches
dangle gleam like beads of morning dew
then they too are fragile and phototropic things.
Have a seat think it over in the long and narrow valley
on the hill stones covered in the green velvet of moss
once I discovered a set of enormous waist-deep footprints
as if a hand accustomed to arranging great affairs
had left proof of itself in an unpredictably tiny way:
such varied measure! A few skeins of glistening web
a few footsteps that made the valley seem like a toy —
listen in the air, the constant zhazha sound of thunder's crush

(1997)

麦芒

MAI MANG

Born in Changde, Hunan Province, Mai Mang (pen name of Yibing Huang; 1967–) was among the youngest students in "Class 83" at Beijing University. His ancestry on his mother's side is from the Tujia ethnic minority, and he has expressed pride in his mixed cultural heritage. In the 1980s he established himself among the mostly highly regarded young poets in Beijing at that time, including Xi Chuan, Xi Du, Hai Zi, Zang Di, and Ge Mai.

After receiving BA, MA, and PhD degrees in Chinese literature from Beijing University, he moved to the United States in 1993, earned a second PhD (from UCLA, in comparative literature), and essentially disappeared from China's national poetry scene.

Since 2000 he has been teaching Chinese literature at Connecticut College. In 2005, he published two poetry collections, *Stone Turtle: Poems 1987–2000,* and *Approaching Blindness,* and in 2007 a book of literary criticism, *Contemporary Chinese Literature: From the Cultural Revolution to the Future.* He served on the jury for the 2010 Neustadt International Prize for Literature and nominated Duo Duo for that award. He has now returned to China as a strong voice, winning the Rou Gang Prize in 2012.

Including Mai Mang in this anthology calls for a complex decision: how do we define Chinese Poetry, categorically? For many years, authors such as Ha Jin (pen name of Jin Xuefei, who won the National Book Award in the United States for his 1999 novel *Waiting*), were excluded from the canon of Chinese literature, because of their foreign citizenship and their chosen language for writing and publishing. In Ha Jin's case, gradually and quietly his work has become a main focus of research and study among scholars who focus on "Overseas Chinese Literature."

And yet poets such as Mai Mang, Xue Di, and others who live and work in the Americas or Europe — and who respond through their writing more to poetic and political issues in China than to aspects of life among the émigrés — have been neglected in both homeland and immigrant communities, although their writings are an important part of contemporary Chinese poetry, enriching and bringing new dimensions to the art.

While the solemn side of Mai Mang may be better known, perhaps because of his solid reputation as an academic sinologist, the more lyrical and playful characteristics of his nature that tend to be overlooked are evident in the poems presented here.

In My Lifetime ...

... I want to encounter one earthquake
One war and two or three imprisonments
On an unnamed square boulevard
A smile from a woman dressed in blue

I want to drink two or three cups of coffee or tea
One bottle of liquor and countless beers
And also taste the kisses said to be harmful to the heart
Paying the price with my youth and a couple of love poems

When I am thirty I want to marry and have a family
Let my beloved feel happy, let children
(If they could really come out into the world)
Remember their irresponsible father

I want to get up early one time to see the rosy clouds of dawn
Speak out loudly in French: "Bonjour"
I want to stay on the balcony for one whole day
I want to idly scratch my head

(1990)

Question and Answer

"Woman, your lips are full
    Can you tell me, me, a stranger
    What kind of future I have here?"

    — I like her smile
A golden gecko

"Stranger, I tell you, your future
    Was written in a book long ago
    But you will not read it soon"

    — Her smile likes me
But I don't plan to hurt her husband

(2006)

蓝蓝

LAN LAN

Lan Lan (pen name of Hu Lanlan; 1967–) was born in Shandong, grew up in Henan, and now lives in Beijing. Her popularity has grown in recent years, as she has won a number of poetry awards in China. Her poems are usually short, made of brief phrases, and yet they have a captivating urgency and startling imagery. Lan Lan looks beyond the pettiness of daily life, writing about nature, death, and other important matters outside the domestic sphere. Although a woman and mother, she leaves her laundry out of the poems and instead seeks a purer role for art. While she occasionally writes about specific events, most of the time she produces abstract mental "paintings," using sharp language and intense rhythms to penetrate a reader's mind.

Wind

The wind blows away what's in his body.

A wooden bridge. Dew on sparrow grass, a lamp at night.
An arm   a face   and in the eyes —
a forest of dandelions.
The wind blows a canyon in his body.
An empty house. Muffled voices
cling to the walls for years.

The wind blows his organs away   the horizon
of his loves. The wind empties him
little by little, making him sand   a pool of dust,
the wind makes him live on —

(2001)

姜涛

JIANG TAO

One of the finest poets in China today, Jiang Tao (1970–) is appreciated more and more by readers and by other writers. Featured as an emerging poet in the past in several international anthologies, his artistic maturity and importance in contemporary Chinese poetry now demands serious study by critics as well as the attention of poets from other countries.

Jiang Tao was born in Tianjin. He obtained a BS in biomedical engineering from Qinghua (Tsinghua) University in 1994 and a PhD in Chinese literature from Beijing (Peking) University, where he has been teaching since 2002. He also serves as an editor for "New Poetry Review," a prominent quarterly journal of poetry criticism in China.

He started writing poetry as a college student in the 1990s and was one of the founding editors for the campus poetry magazines "Offset" and "Poetry Communications." He became known in the late 1990s and his popularity rose when his first collection of poetry, *Bird Sutras,* was published in 2005. Prior to that publication, he was known mainly as a poetry critic. He won a national prize for "Outstanding Achievement in Doctoral Dissertation" (2004) for *The Rise of Modern Poetry in China,* and his collection of critical essays *The Hands of Bakunin* was published in 2010. He has also edited "Beijing University Literary Forum," "Poetry Reader" (for college students), "Appreciation of Foreign Poetry & Prose," and "An Anthology of 20th Century New Verse" (Volume 1); and he has translated Marston Anderson's *The Limits to Realism: Chinese Fiction in the Revolutionary Period* (2001).

Jiang Tao's poetry is marked by an understatement and irony; although seemingly detached from current social life, meanwhile he is criticizing many aspects of society using the "masks" of retired workers, young factory girls, or homebound guys. This reliance upon multiple personas sometimes makes his poetry seem indirect, but this approach brings out diverse perspectives and

varied voices, which has influenced other poets of Jiang Tao's gen-
eration in China. His complex use of tones, including sly mocking
or casual ridicule, is presented obliquely but hits strongly, often
with more impact than direct criticism would.

A Homebound Guy

Somehow I've picked up a not disastrous habit
of walking along a small railway and saying hullo in Esperanto
when I meet a yellow dog.
Occasionally a tram passes by through whose windows
I glimpse white-collar beauties
and guess which have been harassed for years.

Well-tended flowers and plants by the roadside
and convenient public toilets built with local taxes,
but on either side two parties stand
sweating and swearing, giving an old partyless bully
a chance to drive the future of this humming city.

I haven't lived here long, not interested in having a share
in the future either — what can I leave behind
with my small casual lifestyle?
So I dream of running into a big fire, a burglar,
a hideous murder; now the police break in
wearing bullet-proof vests and order me to surrender,
but I gasp for air
speaking in a hoarse voice with a foreign accent.
So I'm arrested, humiliated,
kept hooded, made to appear on television,
prosecuted with great fanfare, then quietly withdrawn,
sent on an airplane, extradited to a foreign land of tyranny

where people walk and sleep smugly and triumphantly.
A few exiles have grown gray early —
they are fond of singing "A Drifting Soul"
after a few drinks.

(2010)

The Tribe of Apes

Fruit falls all over the forest, a bloody carpet
laid down when the earth shifted
Now the water has receded, and the tigers' saber teeth have rotted,
we gather around a clearing to discuss our future
The elderly crawl out of evolution, waving wrinkled fists
and the younger ones can't hold their tongues, eager
to feast on the Sika deer, splashing through the low water
with no desire to "move mountains." From North to South,
the whole field is a dining table
The "Republic" mutters, while the dictators
chase after mosquitoes and flies
Fortunately we all stand upright, able to see easily
what's coming, to break the shackles of the food chain
But our efforts in October tend to produce
surplus: we don't need face-painting, cooking or
to use flesh as lumber, only males overthrowing females
continuously while chanting their animal-beauty
But to speak the words I love you will take at least
another two million years
of spring cherries and autumn moons

(2003)

The Afternoon I Started Teaching

A huge crowd of darkness —
so how is it that I can so easily identify
male and female, decent and evil, insects and aliens?
Time indulges itself,
tongueing slowly from my left cheek to my right.
When it stops, the class ends, the platform descends
like a cliff.

So, this is the world, larger than I thought.
Under every leaf
hides a pair of students shoplifting kisses. On the famous lake
the color of pee (although not famous for that)
float large graves.

You don't need to be prepared,
just open your mouth and you'll be transformed
— you're actually always ready. But
according to an incoming text message
my evolution, not so easy, needs to start from a winged insect.

(2007)

POETRY AND REALITY

Six years ago, I came here
with a clean face and fresh lungs
looking around, non-stop,
and caused a car to crash into the hillside.
The driver, a local Tibetan, was arrested by the police.
I heard the roar of the river below
and people cried out in the mountains:
What are you here for?
But I didn't have a family then, nor a house,
nor more than ten years of serious study.
How could I answer?
So they made me drink non-stop
and tell a couple of jokes from the interior
but the air was too thin, I stammered
like a stone rolling down the snowy mountain
rolling into the car
and rolling back to Beijing.
There were many circles in Beijing, I was shy,
poor, and my girlfriend was deeply depressed
so I chose to live outside the five rings.
Since then, everything has just happened.
The air is fresh in the neighborhood,
everything's greenified, even people, neighbors
are mostly salt-of-the-earth, no elites,
I watch TV to know what's going on.
These past six years, the country's had its ups and downs.
Has all that development out west come to nothing?
Railroads have brought in more backpackers,
more Sichuan girls on the way.
They're also enraptured, they vomit as well,

dreaming too of their homes rising three thousand meters high,
but they're honest, don't ask questions,
fate and dollar bills are bound together.
Six years gone in a flash.
The very best of them
most likely by now have slept together.

(2008)

蒋浩

JIANG HAO

With his classical flavors and subtleties, Jiang Hao (1971–) is distinct among his peers. A stone, a boat, a friend visiting or leaving, a pet that has just died … in his well-crafted poems, every little detail leads to retrospection, with a Daoist outlook. Jiang Hao is a poet with a strong sense of "responsibility" to the tradition; as he states, "There was too much Western influence in Chinese poetry in the 1970s and '80s. Starting from my generation, things should change."

A poet, essayist, and book designer, Jiang Hao was born in Chongqing, Sichuan Province. He wandered around the country, working on various writing or editorial jobs, and eventually he settled in Hainan Island (also known as South Sea Island), off China's southern coast. He has published one volume of essays and three poetry collections, and he has edited "New Poetry," a book-like magazine.

"The Shape of the Ocean" was translated into English in 2009, the original poem having been written in 2003 on Hainan Island. Like contemporaries who have brought traveling into their poetry, Jiang Hao has written many poems embodying his experiences passing through Sichuan, Hainan, Xinjiang, Beijing, and many other parts of China. He moves around in a continual search for meanings. What's interesting about "The Shape of the Ocean" is that it's about the poet's home territory and yet applies to everywhere, everyone. Is it possible to discover life's true meaning from its surface or shape? Each little object tells you something about a certain aspect of life but not all of life.

When facing the ocean or the moon or a landscape, ancient poets lamented the passing of time. Contemporary poets try to escape sentimentality and claim to face "new realities."

In this poem Jiang Hao is not searching for one answer; he is not affirming or denying anything. He doesn't need absolute answers. He is looking for something that looks like fish but is not fish, or is fish but not called fish, or is non-fish that's called fish. His diction is clearly Daoist, which can look and sound almost ungrammatical in modern Chinese. Although sometimes criticized as pedantic or "over-educated" by people who feel confused by a first reading of his work, Jiang Hao is praised by many others who appreciate the classical resonance of his poetry.

THE SHAPE OF THE OCEAN

Every time you ask about the shape of an ocean
I should bring you two bags of ocean water.
This is ocean's shape, like a pair of eyes,
or the shape of ocean that eyes have seen.
You touch them, as if wiping away
two burning tears, as tears
are the ocean's shape, too, the clarity
springing from the same soul.
Putting the bags together will not
make the ocean wider. They are still fresh,
as if two non-fish will soon swim out.
You sprinkle the water to the sand of flour,
the bread, also, is the shape of the ocean.
Before you slice it with a sharp sail
it leaves, like a departing boat. The plastic bags
left on the table also have the ocean's shape, flat
with tides retreating from the beaches.
When the real tide goes away,
there's salt left, shaped as the ocean too.
You don't believe? I should bring you a bag
of water and a bag of sand, the shape of ocean.
You affirm, you deny; then you non-affirm,
and non-deny? Go on and try out yourself,
as this is your shape too. But you say
"I'm only the image of myself."

(2003)

A PEBBLE

The air is clean after a shower,
a pebble at the foot of a tree
also clean, speckled with
rain. Maybe I'll sit
on it again, for half an hour only,
leaving time for birds, lizards, geckos,
and even squirrels to sit, and watch
the sea, as the pebble gets
rounder, the surface smooth
and glossy like an egg floating
on the fallen leaves
on the white sands. The pebble
is an egg
laid by the tree, waiting
to be hatched, I think. A branch,
tilted and hanging above,
like a young snake creeping
out of its egg,
swings its tiny legs as if
to kick the empty pebble
into the sea. (To be hatched?)

(2003)

from BOOK OF SIN

1.

I dream of things, and they grow tall — looking down
at dreams. After June, a new hoe awaits you, covered with
dragonflies. Those who have fallen there drag your shadow around
in the water. Rippled. That's you, walking, in the ridge between the
thread-bound books, laboring. Dust shivers, but not stirring me

or the old wheels under the eaves. When time wakes up,
you point to the spider and the bat: "The messengers of Day and Night
must love each other, as rice and wheat falling from the sky."
Dew, shaken loose by mustaches, makes the star-chasing meadow mice
stoned in the grass. Light creeps to the treetops. How can I imagine
        you completely

and see myself clearly? "Am I still the son you needed?"
You keep the flames and let the last batch of butterflies fly away
bypassing the altar. I lie down by the locust tree, reading birds in the sky.
Like smoke rising and spiraling from different villages, we finally
        embrace in the air.
And is that you? Reaching out for the sun in the water, like finding
        a china bowl

with gold rim, smashed in the early years. Night smells of herbal medicine,
someone by the well signs. The moon splits the black hair.
"It's time. A person has only a fleeting presence.

You may repent, make life lower its wings, and lay your body flat."
But you stand. A green vegetable coughs to itself and beats its chest
        with leaves.

(1995; *excerpt from a long poem*)

吕约

Lü Yue

Lü Yue (1972–) may first strike readers with her "journalistic" approach to poetry, as she discusses current issues and events while simultaneously using bold comedy and irony to criticize conventions and traditions. Lü Yue's language is complicated on other levels, too. As literary critic Zhu Dake has noted, her play on the multiple meanings of Chinese idioms creates effects like the "irregular stripes on tigers that [make] reading confusing and enjoyable at the same time."

Lü Yue was born in Hubei. After graduating in 1993 from East China Normal University in Shanghai with a major in Chinese literature, she went to Guangzhou for a teaching job and then moved to Beijing. She is now the vice chief editor of the capital city's "New Beijing," a dynamic newspaper where she has worked for a number of years as a journalist and editor.

As a journalist-poet, in her poems Lü Yue uses short, news-like phrases and a detached tone for dramatic impact. Little details add up, developing to an outcome. Her poetry has humor and even sarcasm, which many poets in the "Spoken Language" group in China have employed since the 1980s, but Lü Yue's wit is distinctively nuanced. She is neither continuing the traditions from earlier poets nor reactively breaking away but rather discovering a fresh language in the common daily speech.

As praised by Chinese poet and independent publisher Shen Haobo, Lü Yue has "a broader perspective and profound sense of history, and she carefully builds an intriguing structure with worldwide themes, embodying a humanistic outlook. She is patient, persistent, moving slowly with a richness of voices, and she is ambitious, taking aesthetic adventures and exploring new forms of expression ..."

In 2012 Lü Yue was the co-winner with Yang Jian (1967–) of the first annual Luo Yihe Poetry Prize, an award in honor of poet-critic-editor Luo Yihe (1961–1989).

IMPERIAL ENVOYS

The newly appointed Chair
of Environmental Protection pounded the table
at the meeting, tears in his eyes:
"No matter who he is, no matter how well
he has performed, how hard his cock is,
he who undermines environmental protection
will be finished!"
Six months later he
was finished

Because by beating on the table
he persecuted the entire forest
Not to mention that the table
was made of the last tree in our country
Not to mention that he splattered saliva
a waste of water resources

The woodpecker serves as the new imperial envoy
taking charge overnight
to carve the judgment of his crimes
on every stump in the woods

(2006)

Sleep Can Never Be Inherited

Our parents sleep soundly
As soon as they say *yes*
or *no*
they start snoring

We can't fall asleep
Even on spring nights
we're restless
tossing questions back and forth
worried about right and wrong,
are we doing what's best?
Even when we close our eyes and stay silent
we're thinking of
how to sneak a peek at the answer sheet

On the other side of the yellow wooden walls
our children
don't sleep at all
sometimes, without warning
they burst out laughing

(2010)

Birthday Incident

Things went uneventfully
on November 5th, my birthday
We were singing playing eating drinking
before dark
One more hour to hang on
till its successful ending

Just when they lit the candles for me to make a wish
out of the blue, it was suddenly announced on TV
"Saddam Hussein will be hanged
for crimes against humanity"

In the middle of blowing out the candles
I'm compelled instead
to choose quickly
whether to make a wish for Saddam
or for the rest of humanity
otherwise it will be exposed
that when it comes to Saddam and humanity
I don't care more for one than the other

"This is a crime against birthdays"
I declare in the darkness

(2006)

Poetry Doesn't Know It's Dead

Poetry doesn't know that it's dead.
A state funeral is taking place on a 1,000-hole golf course,
its eyelids are sprinkled with petals, and on the petals a few teardrops,
one from Greek, one from Latin
and the rest from crocodiles.
An epitaph is written in Chinese oracle script.
All that have two legs have witnessed its death, it died finally
shrouded in black and gold,
its mouth faintly grinning.

Grasshoppers are alive, so are lizards and butterflies.
All that crawl or fly are alive.
Dinosaurs are walking to the zoo with children for a spring outing,
their small bellies bulging with fresh milk.
The Pope is alive, on his way to Africa by air.
Africa is alive.
Robots of the ninth generation will be alive too.
Poetry is dead, but doesn't know it yet.
Still dreaming of parachuting in heaven with all the living,
small or pregnant.
Still dreaming of shooting off rockets.
Of running marathons in the Third World streets
with a bulletproof vest.

In the funeral a child sees poetry still rolling its eyes
under its lids.
It has donated its corneas —
it will never see its own death

(2007)

SITTING

All creatures with bottoms
no wings
sit
They need to sit
love to sit
have to sit
must sit
They sit comfortably, sit elegantly
sit solemnly
sit steadily
they've forgotten they were not able to sit
at birth
The vertebrate animals can't sit, nor the ones with shells
The first to sit down
paid in blood
They knocked their teeth on the backs of chairs
and became sworn brothers
with the chairs
and confidants with all
who can sit
Whatever door they open, they immediately
look with one eye
for the one sitting
and with the other for a chair
wishing all the chairs would flirt with them
The warmest chair comes up by itself
asks you to sit down and gives you a yellow cushion

The friendliest one coughs
or nods his head

implying that you may take a seat
You both believe that
whether you sit down to polish shoes, go fishing or bite nails
once you sit down
an opportunity will come
Writing poetry requires sitting
Negotiation requires sitting
To issue an order requires sitting
The most enjoyable thing is to sit in someone else's lap
But it won't last long
Because he'll worry that you'll eventually want to sit on his head

Saying "Right" or "Wrong" while sitting
is more powerful
than saying it while standing
Some people will immediately run to deliver what you want
to those standing or kneeling
It might be a little inconvenient to sit
But it's enough to make it hard for others to breathe

It's dangerous if
everybody is seated
and only you stand
It's much better when everyone stands and only you sit
But that is dangerous too

Walking or running is to look for answers
lying down is to give up on answers
But sitting means you know where to get the answers
as sitting is the answer itself

Beloved friends
I remember your sitting postures
You sit pretty
steady
To sit down means to have power
To sit down implies strength
From a sitting position
to suddenly stand up
also produces a force
But the force is not comparable
to sitting all the time

What the most powerful one fears most
is when an enemy takes a chair
and sits in front of him
The only people who do not fear are children
because they don't like to sit down

It's also a kind of power to sit on the street corner waiting for no one
To sit by a grave is another power
To sit on a toilet is the weakest power
To sit in meditation like a monk seeking nirvana —
is that the greatest power?
To sit in a portrait
in Panjia market waiting for the highest bid
from a wealthy man from Dubai —
this is the highest state attainable
But what if a child refuses to sit down
and sets fire to the portrait?

Sitting, the tail is tucked under the buttocks
This changes the body and blood type
The legs become shorter, feet smaller
The belly and head bigger and bigger
like the half-bodies in a deck of cards
The energy and ignorance from their birth
grow while they're sitting

You sit down to nod
Sit down to count money
Sit down to make love
Sit down to kill, sit down to do make up
Sit down to wait for death to come
And you may forget that you can fly while sitting
You sit on a high chair,
launching yourself out
using gunpowder from the Shang dynasty or the Yangtze #8 rocket
You land in a crater in the southeast corner of Pluto
When you land you remain in a sitting position

If you maintain that posture to the final moment
God will bring you a chair
let you sit in front of him
and the other creatures will not say a thing
In the hallway outside the offices of God
they stand, squat, lie on their backs, lie on their bellies
Their eyes are lifeless
like a bunch of pebbles
They seem to be sitting, but aren't really sitting

They try to beat those who are sitting as if they're really sitting.
They punish those sitting
and make them pay tax
Or force them to sit in a ring and sing kindergarten songs
Are they coming up with a scheme?

Some sit so straight
as if there's no need at all for sitting

(2007)

胡续冬

HU XUDONG

Hu Xudong (1974–) was born in Sichuan Province and moved to Hubei Province in his teenage years. He attended college and graduate school at Beijing University, where he currently teaches Portuguese literature. He has also taught abroad, as visiting professor at University of Brasilia (Brazil) (2003–2005), fellow at the International Writing Program at University of Iowa (2008), poet-in-residence at the Hermitage Artist Retreat in Florida (2008), and visiting professor at the National Central University of Taiwan (2010). He has published six books of poetry and several collections of essays.

If resistance to the central establishment in China brought changes to the literary scene in the 1970s, and western literature brought new ideas in the 1980s and '90s, the new age is facing new voices from poets who have traveled and lived in countries outside China. Hu Xudong, Zang Di, Xiao Kaiyu, and others have brought their experiences of foreign lands into their writing and they keep exploring different ways of doing so. These are not poets in exile, and they do not have political agendas; they simply want to make poetry more interesting.

If you think Hu Xudong's "Mama Ana Paula Also Writes Poetry" is frivolous, you are far from understanding the new generation of writers in China. If you think Hu Xudong is making fun of this woman Ana Paula, you are even farther away from grasping the values of China's "New Poetry." And if you think he's saying that you can't judge people by their appearance, then you may not understand the mechanisms of poetry at all. Hu Xudong has been criticized by some for not writing seriously enough, but he is highly regarded by his peers for his hilarity, irony, insightfulness in observation, originality in imagery, and innovative use of language. He is one of the most exciting poets in China today.

LIFE-LONG UNDERCOVER

What planet are you from, stranger?
You have an outer-space violin in your left ear
that plays a string of quiet clouds
in the noisy subway.
I suspected it, and others, too, suspected it
and, true: you have a strange device on your retina
that can always catch the small ads falling from the sky
through the windy air down to the streets.
Even the sleeping fats in your body are suspiciously
beautiful.
I worry that one day you will
wing your way back to that other planet with the potato chips
that are left in your hands decorating your big wings.
And I will be left here alone trying to decipher
your space diary written in snow.
I worry. I always worry.
Fortunately: I've snapped a wavelength of your planet
by pulling out a poetic antenna
in the back of my head
while you are cooking in the kitchen.
You are cooking again, this morning.
A little voice of alien vowels issues an order
to the woodpecker
five meters
from our balcony: Let her stay there
as our life-long
undercover
       his side, do not try to wake her up!

MAMA ANA PAULA ALSO WRITES POETRY

A tobacco of corn husks in mouth, she throws a thick poetry book
at me, "Read your Mama's poems."
This is true, my student
José's mother,
two Brazils on her chest, a South America on her bucks,
a stomach full of beer, surging like Atlantic,
this Mama Ana Paula
writes poetry. The first day I met her, she lifted me
up like an eagle
catching a small chicken, I wasn't informed She Writes Poetry.
She spat at me her wet words, and rubbed
my face
with her big palm tree fingers. When she licked my
panicked ears
with marijuana tongue, I didn't know She Writes Poetry.
Everyone including her son José and daughter-in-law Gisele said
she was an old Flower Silly, but no one
told me She Writes Poetry.
"Put my teacher down, my dear old Flower Silly." José said.
She dropped me, but went on
vomiting "dick" "dick," and catching "dick"
in the air with her lips. I looked at her
back, strong like hairy bear that kills
a bull even when she's drunk, and I understood:
She Writes Poetry.
But today, when I followed José into the house, and caught a glimpse
of her lying by the pool
with four limbs stretched out, smoking, I didn't think She Writes Poetry
I ran into a ponytail
like Bob Marley, a muscle guy, in the living room, Gisele told me

that's her mother-in-law's guy from last night, I didn't think, even if
you stick me in front of a National Army of China and shoot at my little
torso, that Mama Ana Paula
writes poetry. But Mama Ana Paula
Mama Ana Writes Poetry Paula
writes poetry
which burps and farts. I leafed it through page after page
Mama Ana Paula's poetry book. Yes, Mama Ana Paula writes poetry
indeed. She doesn't write fat poetry, liquor poetry,
marijuana poetry, dick poetry, or muscle poetry of muscle guys.
In a poem called "Three Seconds of Silence in Poetry"
she wrote: "Silence in a poem, give me a minute and in it
I can spin the nine yards of sky."

(2004, Brasilia)

Humpback Whale

Two huge clouds droop from the sky
onto the ocean surface
and in that cleavage, a small fishing boat—
with a little steering it sprouts wings
and flies out
to chase seagulls,
drawing a new coastline.
The road is spiraling uphill,
lifting the ocean.
When we're near the top, my thin retina
can't embrace the ocean that looks heavy and dull
as my aged ancestors. I close my eyes.
Inside the car, the air-conditioning blows out
piano fingers of cold air that play my arms
in recurrent invisible waves.
Under my skin streams out a large pod of humpback whales
raising their heads, spewing out
farewell to me, as solemn as the standard scripts of the island.

(2010, Taiwan)

PAPER-BOAT INCENSE

In Memory of Ma Hua and Ma Yan*

Two years ago I found this paper-boat incense
in Double Village
west of Lake Peng in Taiwan Island,
but the two of you were already
gone —
one in the sky making white clouds into snow mountains,
the other catching gusts of dust
from the deep night.

You are both far, in that high place,
with Mandarin wings.
The way you travel forward
is becoming a long poem, one light-year long.
Stars are reading you.
Perhaps you visit each other and take out
the treasured time from your wings
and share with each other.
The two of you, if you can really
meet up there, perhaps you can share how we miss you
from down here — we miss you
like a memory that doesn't know how to bear itself.

The sky is open blue for you
today. You
tipple a little wine, grin,
and the sky blooms — in its own distances.

Let me light an incense for you,
the Double Village paper-boat incense,
let it burn,
burn out two beams of light.
There are no rivers or oceans in that high place,
but still,
may your young bodies surge like full sails puffed with wisdom.

Now I notice the words printed on the paper boat,
"Brave guys don't leave."
And this is exactly what I wanted to say.
If you didn't go, if you didn't go …

(2012)

* *Translators' note: Ma Hua and Ma Yan (not related; Ma is a common Chinese family name) were two of the most loved poets in contemporary China, and both died young in recent years.*

GRASSHOPPERS

Walking. Walking alone in despair.
The massive autumn tiger is roaring above me,
a God in pseudonym.
Countless autumn tigers
hide in the numerous motor vehicles on the road,
howling from their gas throats
as if in chorus, scolding me, the only creature without gas
on the road.
I feel guilty, a happy sensation, a thrill of crime.
Yes, I'm walking on the highway
with a weighted backpack on my shoulders and firm steps
in the wilderness outside this little town.
No bus routes run between the two shopping centers
and I definitely don't look like a shopper
picking underwear for my distant wife.
I'm a suspicious guy with sun burns,
and poison milk powder, bombs, or communism
in my backpack.

My footsteps awaken some other creatures
on the roadside, who have no gas in their bodies either
just like me; grasshoppers. They live a small life
in this huge country.
They are fantastic country musicians.
Their little wings and back legs make friction
that takes me back to the rice fields of the Sichuan Basin
from this gigantic North American prairie.
Come on grasshoppers, sing your little songs

before I die from sweating too much.
Put all the autumn tigers
to sleep and let me walk my way alone.

(2008, Iowa City)

亦来

YI LAI

Yi Lai (pen name of Zeng Wei; 1976–) was born in Zhijiang, Hubei Province, graduated from Central China University with a BS in Computer Science and a PhD in Comparative Literature and World Literature, and now serves as the vice chief editor of the university press at his alma mater. He is the only poet in this anthology who lives in Hubei, the central part of China, home of Qu Yuan — the earliest known of China's ancient poets. We have introduced poets from Beijing (in the north), Heilongjiang (northeast), Zhejiang (east), Fujian (southeast), Guangdong and Hainan (south), and Sichuan (west). Yi Lai not only fills a geographical gap, he represents a different type of writing — he's one of the finest Chinese poets to emerge in the Internet age.

He started writing poetry in his undergraduate years and was among those young poets very active on the internet in the late 1990s and early twenty-first century. In those years his work was widely published in print and on the web, and he was known nationwide, but suddenly in the mid-2000s he voluntarily withdrew from the Internet, choosing to publish only in "Pictographic," a private annual publication established in 2006 in the capital of Hubei, which became known throughout the country by 2008 and still publishes today with a strong reputation.

Yi Lai believes that good poetry comes from writing for a few friends instead of for a mass audience. "Pictographic" was created when a group of Hubei poets gathered for drinks and to exchange new poems. They have continued to gather regularly, critiquing each other's work and publishing together once a year in their collective annual. "Pictographic" — the name indicates a yearning to return to the old tradition, as the Chinese language has evolved from pictographic writing. But Yi Lai's poetry is firmly anti-traditional. He has adopted the Chinese classical rhetoric, but he questions every aspect of literary convention and challenges the usual perspectives on life.

Darkroom

Hah, what a sultry profession.
In the darkroom he becomes what he sees —
a peach, a butterfly, or a flying bird.
If he sees a garden he will feel rain
in his left eye while on his right knee
many little creatures rise from hibernation.
He never has doubt about his vision, as he trusts
the lens that makes judgment of life.
He knows for sure that Spring is here —
there is bright light outside, and a dazzling young girl
in the park, or on a T-shaped platform.
(Here comes his fantasy.)
He knows she will take off her hat, then her scarf,
and will watch out for pollen or mosquitoes.
All this knowledge comes from the process of developing
and restoring things to their originals, or to "more than likely,"
like what we learn from books about optics.
In the tons and tons of films he even thinks that he owns
a whole pipeline of Spring.
But when he tries to finds his body —
all he sees is a small bit of darkness.

(2001)

江离

JIANG LI

Jiang Li (pen name of Lü Qunfeng; 1978–) was born in the Zhejiang Province of eastern China. His childhood experience of growing up with parents in two locations is not unusual in many parts of China, where parents often live separately due to the difficulty of obtaining household registrations in the cities. Jiang Li lived with his mother in the countryside while his father worked in the city, the family coming together only on weekends. When he was twelve, his father became terminally ill and died less than a year later. This memory and his early awareness of death haunt his poetry. Yet what makes his poems shine is their quiet meditative tone and the ways he relates personal feelings to broader questions of human existence.

Jiang Li started writing poetry in high school and became seriously engaged in the 2000s. In 2002, he was a founding editor of "Out in the Field," an independent magazine devoted to younger poets in China and world-class poets in other countries. Under the aegis of this magazine he co-hosted monthly discussion salons. In 2004, he earned a master's degree in philosophy from Zhejiang University, and in 2008 he became an editor for *Jiang Nan* magazine. When his first collection of poems was published, he was recognized as an emerging poet of exceptional quality. In 2011 he became chief editor of *Poetry Jiang Nan* ("Poetry South of the River") and a co-founding editor of "Poetry Construction" with Quan Zi (both publications are influential in central and eastern China).

Jiang Li lives away from the capital, historical center of the poetry establishment, and away from the new century's noisy Internet poetry scene. Still, he has remained devoted to poetry, making contributions and having a significant impact on contemporary Chinese writing.

Jiang Li's "An Old Woman's Timepiece" alludes to an important Chinese poet in the 1990s, Xi Du (1967–), who published a long poem entitled "Memory from a Watchmaker" (1997), in which he wrote from the perspective of a watchmaker about a young girl coming of age and going through life until death. Jiang Li's poem is about an old woman seen from the perspective of her children. In writing about her loneliness after the loss of her beloved, Jiang Li doesn't merely observe the woman and her life, but also uses her circumstances as the jumping-off point for deeper ruminations, moving beyond the personal realm.

SEARCHING

Halfway there, we begin to regret.
The sky looks like a dangerous house, then it starts
to rain, and the rain seems like dandruff falling
before the headlights, causing us more distress.
It's hard to find the address.
Everybody shakes their head when asked, making us
even more doubtful.
The vehicle is moving forward slowly, stopping
from time to time. People behind us honk their horns.
The roadside pedestrians in rain-gear enter
our side mirror, draining our last reserves.
When we settle into a small inn at night
fatigue floods over us. We huddle in
our dreams, realizing what we tried to find
was only a dried matchbox ·

(2002)

GEOMETRY

For Cai Tianxin

After the snow storm, I move to the mountaintop
and stroll among the blue and white stars
every evening. Houses move slowly
like caravans in the desert, a decrepit orange color
that we've never seen in the woods.
A neighbor grown distant is gone.
I worry, and even my worry seems superfluous.
In my notebook, I faithfully record
births, deaths,
and the delicate balance in between.
There seems to be a structure: each of them exists
in another. Solitude
must become part of a greater friendship.
And for immortality, time must be re-divided.
In my room, the tables and chairs in chaos
form another expression of clarity.

(2002)

An Old Woman's Timepiece

Sometimes we return late at night
and see the lights still on in her room.
How she sets her time, fast or slow,
is like going through a long conversation
again and again. She needs a listener
where she can land, a window
to collect the specimens of solitude.
There is a rotating gyroscope inside people,
a precision instrument
with a tilted axis that you can't get close to,
it's like a glassware of hours:
every word you say goes through a little bending.

(2002)

ETERNITY

On a cold morning, I went to see my
father. In that white room,
he was wrapped in sheets, and there he said,
the only time he spoke, remember, he said,
remember these faces — nothing can keep them.
Yes, I've borne them in mind.
But in fact my father said nothing.
He lay there, face covered in white. He had died.
But for a long time he didn't disappear.
As always, he ordered me around, here, there,
in a tone unique to the dead,
he asked me to find immortality in things perishable
— the only things immortal.
Am I awake? It's as if I wasn't born from the womb
but from the death.
All right, listen to me, everything ends here now.
For fourteen years, I've never caught the essence
of things, only emptiness,
and the emptiness in its various forms.

(2005, 2007)

郑小琼

ZHENG XIAOQIONG

The poetry of Zheng Xiaoqiong (1980–) exploded on the Chinese literary scene in 2007 when she won the prestigious Liqun Literature Award from "Peoples' Literature." The impact was unexpectedly strong because few people had heard of her, and even more so because she lives and works as a migrant laborer and she writes poetry so startlingly beautiful and powerful that nearly each poem stops one's breath mid-line.

Born in rural Sichuan Province, in 2001 in search of work Zheng Xiaoqiong moved to Dongguan City in southern Guangdong Province, and she began to write poetry during a six-year stint in a hardware factory.

While some critics have tried to pigeonhole Zheng Xiaoqiong as a "migrant worker poet," her poetry defies the aesthetic expectations this label would imply. At one level she depicts the painful vulnerability of migrant workers within the grind of factory life, but she does so by evoking an industrial pastoral where machines, fire, and above all "iron" convulse around the workers in a terrifying sublime.

Stylistically her work is quite complex: readers will be confronted by intricate syntactical enjambment and ambiguity of images within and between the lines, as well as copious references to classical Chinese history, literature, and philosophy. This combination makes her work hard if not impossible to categorize.

Critic Zhang Qinghua has discussed Zheng's work in more detail in his essay "Who Touches the Iron of the Age: On Zheng Ziaoqiong's Poetry" in the first issue of *Chinese Literature Today* (2010). The poems sampled here may be eclipsed by her subsequent efforts, but these pieces provide at least a glimpse of her range of themes and concerns and language-play.

— *Jonathan Stalling*

INDUSTRIAL ZONES

Lamps burn bright, buildings burn bright, machines burn bright
Fatigue burns bright, blueprints burn bright…
This is Sunday night; this is the night of August fifteenth
The moon is a blank circle; in the lychee trees
A cool breeze sways inside the pure white body, so many wordless years
Silence in the evergreen weeds, insects cry out, the lamps of the whole city
      burn bright
Inside the factories, so many dialects, so much homesickness,
So many frail and skinny workers dwell there, so much moonlight falls upon
Sunday's machines and blueprints. And now it is rising
Shining on my face. Slowly, I am loosing my heart

So many lamps are glaring, so many people passing by
Place yourself inside the bright factories, memories, machines
The speechless moonlight, lamplights, like me
Are so tiny, fragments of spare parts, filaments
Using their vulnerable bodies to warm the factory's hustle and noise
And all the tears, joy, pain we have ever had
Those noble or humble ideas, spirits are
Illuminated, stored up by moonlight, and taken so far
To fade away as unnoticed rays of light

(2011)

from THE COMPLETE DARKNESS

1.

Three fish shoulder daybreak, poetry, Qu Yuan running
Symmetrical snow melts into Li Bai's bones along with the wine
        of Chang'an
The tri-color glazed pottery of the Tang dynasty, the flying frescoed
        apsaras, the terra-cotta warriors advance in lines
A person who will be melted into soil delivers a speech, holding a
        red prayer flag
Dharma passing away, the inborn "four elements," the "six
        combinations" sever the arm
Death is another waking
The bird of time shakes off the emperor's plumage
Along elongated reproductive tracts, bloody elegies move the
        imperial ships
The ghosts of the boatmen upon the River Chuan fall upon
        the paths of Ba Mountain
In the voyeuristic eyes of ethnographers
You caress elemental fire, fire's Great Wall
No nirvanic phoenix. Desires of the flesh
Two men are fighting for. Its stomach
War's meat grinder crushed the imperial dream
History deposits its sanitary napkins along the floor of
        the bleeding River Chuan
Along with antibiotics to stop its menstruation
There are 1.04 million people live with AIDS, and millions
        of prostitutes
To revive the impotent empire with eastern Viagra,

The fleet drifts along the blood vessels of woman
The market's Yin and Yang conspires with the Plan
Giving way to heap of false reports

(2003; *excerpt from a long poem*)

丘启轩

QIU QIXUAN

When asked who's the best poet in China, Qiu Qixuan (1984–) answered "the door-keeper at Industrial University." He is very critical of contemporary Chinese poetry — "too many lofty slogans, too many -ism's, too many circles, too many noises." Together with Zi He and other young poets, Qiu Qixuan edits a poetry publication called "No. 12," a beautifully designed and printed magazine that he refuses to call a magazine, apparently believing that the term is pretensious. He considers himself an anonymous poet, "absent" from poetry. He doesn't read T. S. Eliot or Joseph Brodsky like nearly all other poets do in China today. Instead, he reads Confucius and Laozi. He argues that it's better to not read any poetry criticism in contemporary China because "they don't tell you anything about poetry but their egos."

Born in Shandong, Qiu Qixuan began writing poetry early. After his Chinese schooling, he spent two years in the United States and in 2010 earned an MBA from the University of California – Riverside. Before he returned to China, he took a one-month trip by train across America, stopping at small towns and observing ordinary life there, which changed his perceptions forever.

In 2010 he won the Weiming Poetry Prize from Beijing University. Currently he works in Beijing but stays away from the poetry centers. He's been deeply involved in contemporary Chinese poetry but maintains his stance as an outsider. The most recent issue of "No. 12" has features many outstanding young Chinese poets, including Xiao Shui, Xu Yue, Wang Xiping, Li Hao, and Li Heng, and also features Qiu Qixuan's own long postscript about what he believes poetry is: a slow mental process that captures and transforms initial impressions.

BAT

Moonlight is not for you, but night is

The eaves and tree branches gain a meaning
when you shuttle like a bird
The way you move about is troubling
and your wings baffle those who watch you
But I watch from a bird's direction, thinking you are a bird too
and this is the cruelest natural law of mirror
— I see you in my night
You don't belong to night
but you only appear at night like dreams
I find your existence puzzling
and overwhelming
I can't actually see the shape of your body
or touch your black hairs
I can only sense the height of where you've been
when I wake up —

if I ever find your body in daytime
I would be destroyed by my own absurdity

(2010)

Song of Love

Love will not end
It only starts, and starts again

like the death of an individual
like tomorrow

It creates a heaven when it's in joy, and
leaves praises behind when it's gone, more than hells

Love will not end
It only starts, and starts again

letting more pain squeeze into your heart
to make the old wounds heal halfway

like pressing plants into coal seams continuously
pressing into old materials, deeper and deeper

If only the final flame would burn quietly
with a warm glow to accompany the aging Borges

(2010)

李淑敏

LI SHUMIN

Born in Anhui, at age twelve Li Shumin (1986–) moved to Kashgar in the Uyghur autonomous region of northwest China, and in 2004 began college in Xi-an City, the ancient capital of China; she started writing poetry that same year.

Although she has taken a different approach in her later work, Li Shumin's early poems show a strong influence from her college professor Yi Sha (1966–), one of the representative poets of the "spoken language" school of Chinese poetry, characterized by plain language and the rhythms of colloquial speech. Yi Sha is famous for his poem "Crossing the Yellow River"(1988), in which he writes about "pee" to satirize civilization and history, to celebrate lively speech instead of literary language, and to demonstrate writing about the body rather than the mind.

For her undergraduate studies, Li Shumin took Yi Sha's classes in Xi-an City, including a writing class, then went to Yi Sha's alma mater in Beijing for her graduate studies; she completed her MA in literature at Beijing Normal University in 2012. She presently works as a poetry editor with the independent publisher Iron Squash Books, whose chief editor is Shen Haobo (1976–), who founded the "Lower Body" school of Chinese poetry.

While Li Shumin has been close to two strong literary figures (neither of whom is included in this anthology, due to space limitations), her poetry seems to be more affected by growing up in the isolated Uyghur desert region of northwestern China. In her work we often hear a private voice that talks of inner feelings, as in "Rain," a poem about awakening. But Li Shumin doesn't focus solely on personal experiences; she also writes evocatively about deserts and cities, as in "Strange Kashgar."

Unlike the realistic descriptions of the spoken language poets, what Li Shumin sees in a city is usually dream-like.She considers what the city is, what it was, what it implies, beyond and above mere "reality." For instance, in Beijing she sees a wounded body on the square and sees birds flying to him — she recalls a memory from history that she is too young to have experienced personally.

Li Shumin's particular quality of voice arises from how she deals with her subject matter. She uses unadorned words, in a controlled structure. She doesn't offer an opinion directly, but presents in a fable-like setting what she "sees," creating a surreal world that's rarely found in the writings of other young poets in today's China.

BIRDS FLY TO HIS RUINED BODY

White cotton eats his limbs
section by section
His face tight
against the red background
He's taken flight —
but in the end
is flown into a huge controlled world
where words river
then choked by mud
On his wounded body flying birds cluster
— he may be still alive
quickening like the summer

(2010)

新华夏集　当代中国诗选

EDITOR'S INTERVIEWS AND SURVEYS

Editor's Interviews with Poets
(excerpts)

ZANG DI

Where in China did you grow up and how did it affect you in becoming a poet?

Zang Di:

What affected me most was relocation at age five from Beijing to a remote place in Yunnan Province and then to Sichuan Province, in southwest China. My father was sent there in 1966, at the beginning of the Cultural Revolution; my mother took me and my brother there in 1969 to join my father. As a child who couldn't understand the meaning of "cultural revolution" and the meaning of migration, before everything else my body (and its chronic illness) had to learn to adjust to the new environment. And due to that sudden change in life, books became my toys — there wasn't much to do but read in bed during my sick days. I became aware of how my health condition affected my reading in those years: When I was getting better, things on the pages looked dynamic; when I was sick and weak, words were a big spiritual comfort to me. I had a deep personal affection for literature in my childhood, which influenced my later writing.

You wrote about your favorite books and characters in your poem "Childhood Chronicles." What other books affected or "enlightened" you in your early years?

Zang Di:

In March 1977, my parents got their jobs back in Beijing so we returned to the capital. We lived on the east side of the city, where there were many stores for new and used books. In the last two years of the 1970s, bookstores were the most significant highlights of Beijing cultural life. And almost the whole city was crazy about reading. People would stand in line for four to five hours to get a copy of any "foreign literature" translated into Chinese. All that was a huge stimulus to me; I was reading everything available. I particularly liked Strindberg's drama; Chekhov's stories; novels and essays by Romain Rolland; and Walt Whitman's *Leaves of Grass*.

I was surprised that there were things in the world that I couldn't understand, such as "The Waste Land" by T. S. Eliot. If you don't understand Pascal you know why, and you know how to get to him, but T. S. Eliot is different. In the early 1980s I couldn't bear the fact that I wasn't able to get to him, but this didn't lead to any hostility; instead it inspired me to do a serious study of modernist literature, which was an important part of my intellectual growth.

As for personal and emotional growth, I was influenced by Hawthorne's *The Scarlet Letter* and Rousseau's *Confessions*. In philosophy, Sartre and Hume were powerful spiritual sources.

In retrospect, my reading in the early 1980s was a wonderful confusion. It takes deep sympathy to understand that situation in China.

What prompted you into poetry writing? Have you ever stopped for a while, as many other poets in China have done?

Zang Di:
In the fall of 1983, I was admitted to Beijing University and I began to write poetry, due to the poetic atmosphere on the campus. At that time, poetry had a unique political implication for young people: Poetry meant freedom. Writing poetry meant you could begin to make personal choices. At the same time I was also writing fiction and drama. As a matter of fact, my most favorite literary genre was drama. But in the 1980s, plays were strictly controlled by the state, because theater was more influential. So I shifted my energy to poetry writing. From 1983 to now, I've never stopped writing poetry. If I don't produce a poem for a month, then there is a problem. But strictly speaking, I was debating between becoming a poet or a novelist for a while, and in 1989 I finally settled on poetry.

What happened when you wrote "James Baldwin Is Dead"?

Zang Di:
I was rebellious in my high school years and I admired James Baldwin very much, as I took him as my role model for rebelling.

I was reading so widely in the early 1980s that I didn't give a shit about Bei Dao. But of course, for a young student it was bad to be so frivolous. So I kept low-key. In January of 1987 when Baldwin passed away, I wrote the poem and showed it to Xi Chuan, and he said it was good. The poem was published in the Beijing University literary magazine "Venus." The lofty tone was in line with another poem, "In Memory of Paul Klee, a Book Series." I believed that one can change the color and state of the world by acts of personal will and by the power of imagination.

"In Memory of Paul Klee" reminds me of my own growing up in China in the 1970s and '80s. What do you try to say in the last two lines of the poem?

Zang Di:
I was exposed to Paul Klee's paintings and diaries in the '80s at age sixteen. Reading his diaries was a positive, life-changing experience. "I want to humbly kneel down, but in front of whom?" That's his line. This was almost the motto of my youth. Klee's influence came along with my acceptance of Sartre's existentialism and my avid reading of Nietzsche. To kneel down means to be in awe. To kneel down means you know your humble mind has unlimited force and limitations at the same time. "But to whom?" Here the question mark is very important. It means I no longer believe in what I trusted previously; I have to face the world alone, to begin a one-person journey of spiritual searching. I have given up worshipping "idols" and kept it open and uncertain as to whom to worship, so that worshiping ritual becomes an internal power.

The early 1980s was a depressing time for a young man of less than twenty years old. I was hungry and had a radical spirit.

If we skip the time in between, who are you reading most in recent years?

Zang Di:
Deleuze. He's quite radical and subversive but not hostile.

To me, the biggest limitation of Chinese New Poetry is the inability to completely get rid of hostility toward its history.

What's "ideal" poetry to you? Do you think you have achieved your goals?

Zang Di:

I change my mind about "ideal" poetry quite often, but basically, an "ideal" poem should contain sufficient linguistic fun, and if you are lucky enough, should also have insight into life and the beauty within our existence.

I'm a very confident poet with very little ego, so for me it's not too difficult to reach the goal or standard that I set in my mind for an "ideal" poem, to the extent that I succeed so often that I have to refresh my standard constantly. For example, recently in my mind good poetry is written by Paul Muldoon in disguise of an ancient Chinese poet, Tao Yuanming.

Whose work do you like most and why? Have you been influenced by that work?

I like a lot of poets — for instance, T. S Eliot in Xiao Kaiyu, Larkin in Huang Canran, Wallace Stevens in Pan Wei, Blake in Wang Ao, Derrida in Yang Xiaobin, Baudelaire in Qing Ping, and Du Fu in Mallarme — among many reasons, the most important being that they have given a lot of fun to language itself, and in turn this fun becomes the great joy of life. Poetry, after several thousands of years of cross-influence, in the most positive sense is joy of reinventing language.

I like to be influenced. Unlike those who resist influence and are worried about losing their individual voice, I don't have such anxiety. In fact, I welcome others to influence me — anyone who influences me, I will influence back with double intensity. I don't indulge myself in so-called independent thinking, I like what Roland Barthes said: he would rather have Brecht working in his brain. When I write poetry, I don't mind if Dante or Du Fu enters my mind. I'm not worried that my individual voice will be lost if they come to my brain.

What do you think of the poetry movements or trends in China?

Zang Di:

They are like shelves in a supermarket. As far as literary history is concerned, this is a simple way of concise classification. To join a movement or not is a matter of luck. It doesn't make you write better. Likewise, not to join any movement doesn't guarantee that you will be able to write good poetry. I'm not sure if I'm right or wrong about that. But I know that the Du Fu in me always goes to the international post-symbolist gatherings without telling the Shakespeare in me.

There is an argument that there are two starting points of Chinese New Poetry, Hu Shi and Misty poetry. What's your take on this?

Zang Di:
Regarding the origin of the New Poetry, there are many sources and starting points; Hu Shi counts as one for sure, but Misty is certainly not. Guo Moruo, Lu Xun, Bian Zhilin, Ai Qing, and Mu Dan: each of them is an important source.

It depends on where you stand to look at the history.

For example, at the age of twenty, if people tell you Guo Moruo is the origin of the new poetry, you will just accept this. However, at age forty you may want to consider Bian Zhilin as the sole origin of the new poetry.

One day in the spring of 2002 I was thinking that Chinese New Poetry started with Walt Whitman inhabiting Bian Zhilin's body.

Many critics say that current Chinese poetry is "better than before." What's your opinion?

Zang Di:
From my personal perspective, in the 1990s I sensed a completely different type of poetry. For the purpose of assessing Chinese poetry development, I think we need to have a new concept for the period since 1990 — a new period we may call "current" poetry. The notion of this "current" poetry being better than the poetry before is held by many people, but to say just "good" or "bad" may not be fair. We can compare many aspects: linguistic awareness; capability in terms of forms; the ability to handle experience and to respond to previous movements; openness; etc.

Contemporary poetry in the last twenty years or so is better than before for many reasons. One important reason is that we've updated our awareness of "contemporariness" in language. We've changed direction in a new, meaningful way.

How do you feel about the situation of contemporary Chinese poetry as translated into English?

Zang Di:
Not adequate. English translators have found effective ways of translating Chinese ancient poetry, and there is a need to find equally effective ways of presenting Chinese modern/contemporary poetry.

I don't want to complain; I just think we can do something to help.

Translation of Chinese poetry is fragmented. Many good poets have not been translated into English or other languages at all. The "West" seems to have a narrow receptivity to Chinese poetry — they are more interested in the "anti-" themes, which may not be wrong, but has the risk of merely pursuing one political flavor.

BAI HUA

What's the most unforgettable event in your childhood that affected your later writing?

Bai Hua:
The first time I ran away from school, at age nine. Witnessing "Red Guards" in green army uniforms...

Memories of fear, hatred, and love have strangely intertwined in the poetic tensions of my earlier poems, and in my later writings as well.

What inspired you to write poetry?

Bai Hua:
I read Baudelaire's *Les Fleurs du Mal* in 1979 and decided to write poetry. Actually I just read a few poems, translated into Chinese by François Cheng. The poetic form and surprisingly bold expressions strongly stimulated me.

What do you think of poetry movements and poetry circles in China? Do you belong to any, and if yes, have you been influenced by this contact with other writers?

Bai Hua:
Poetry circles can be meaningful. Unfortunately, I didn't have such opportunities earlier on. All I did was form a sort of "Confidante" relationship with Zhang Zao.

In my earlier years I exchanged ideas with Zhang Zao and also Ouyang Jianghe, because we had similar taste in poetry. Zhang Zao and I influenced each other, but we had natural differences.

How do you judge the origin of Chinese New Poetry at the beginning of the last century? How do you evaluate current Chinese poetry almost a hundred years later?

Bai Hua:
Chinese New Poetry was born when Western modernism intervened.

Current Chinese poetry is extremely rich and diversified. I like the hybrid poetry of mixed Europeanization with Chinese classical features.

SONG LIN

What are the biggest concerns for most Chinese poets at the present time?

Song Lin:
I can only briefly talk about a few main issues.

First, to restore the dignity of poetry. There has been a phenomenon of popularizing poetry and making it a kind of entertainment. The public has a low opinion of poetry and poets, and certain low-taste poems have been spoofed on the Internet. As a result, in 2007 some poets proposed a poetic convention of principles: to respect our mother tongue, to witness our time, to understand our traditions, and so on.

Secondly, in October 2008 there was a poetry event in the Yellow Mountains where a dozen Chinese and international poets discussed "How poetry responds to reality."

The third concern I'll mention is locality and historical perspective in writing. The 2012 spring issue of "Today" carried long poems by Bei Dao, Xi Chuan, Ouyang Jianghe, and Zhai Yongming with the common theme of "How poetry responds to history." (Whether this attempt is successful or not is another matter).

Since the late 1970s, meaning the post-Mao era, the core issues — in all the forms of modern or contemporary Chinese poetry — include the relationship between poetry and politics, between tradition and modernity, and between poets and the mother tongue.

What do you think are the best literary journals in China? How would you define "official" and "independent"? What role do independent poetry publications play, and can one find good poems in institutional or "government" journals?

Song Lin:

Unofficial and underground poetry journals have played a huge role in promoting poetry in China. In 1978, Bei Dao and Mang Ke founded "Today." A year later, this journal was forced to suspend publication, but its impact spread across the country. In the 1980s unofficial or independent poetry journals appeared in many parts of China; the most influential were "Make It New," "Them," "Not-Not," and "At Sea." In the 1990s there were "Opposition," "Southern Poetry," "Modern Chinese Poetry," and "Poetry and Poets." In the current century, the most notable journals are "Chinese Poetry Review," "Chinese Poetry," "Poetry Reading," "Poetry East West," and "Poetry Construction."

Personally I was involved in 1982 in starting a campus journal called "Summer Rain Island" in Shanghai (we produced about ten issues) and in 1988 another journal called "Blind Migration" (only one issue). Since 1992 I've been part of the editing team of Bei Dao's "Today" (which in 1992 resumed quarterly publication in Europe). Since 2011 I've also been involved with editing "Poetry Reading" (we've produced six volumes so far).

As for the difference between "government official" poets and "independent" poets, in my opinion this is a matter of self-identity.

Do poetry prizes promote good poetry in China? Is the competition fair? Is there a difference between government-sponsored and private awards?

Song Lin:
There are more and more poetry prizes and awards, some subject to a selection process, some subject to the limitations of a judge's taste. Whether government or private, it's difficult to maintain fairness. If we look at the resulting winners, the private awards seem to be more credible than the government ones. I do not intend to evaluate/criticize specific prizes. I've received a few poetry awards and have been on the selection committees of several private awards.

What's the situation of poetry publication in China? Do poetry books get reviewed regularly?

Song Lin:
Poetry publication is in recession now. Most poets have to self-publish. There is no guarantee of quality. Personal qualification of the editor speaks more than the name of the publishing company. There are no regular reviews.

How is poetry criticism doing in China? Does it have any influence?

Song Lin:
The influence of poetry criticism is confined to colleges of liberal arts. In Shenyang Normal University, where I teach, there are fewer graduate students who pursue a career in literary criticism than in other fields of study.

Many poets claim to be "avant-garde." How would you define "avant-garde" and "experimental" in the context of Chinese poetry?

Song Lin:
"Avant-garde" means politically and aesthetically rebellious, but in contemporary China, simply to stay away from the established ideology isn't sufficient to reflect the true essence of being "avant-garde." Individualistic or "private" writing is not effective, due to the urgency to face society and promote conscience in writing.

"Experimental" refers to openness in texts and the revitalizing of language. Different poets have different approaches, in terms of using spoken or written language, or a mixture of classical and contemporary dictions, dialects, slangs, or Westernized syntax, etc., which present different aesthetics.

Experimental writing to the extreme of abandoning ethics would exhaust the poetic beauty of language.

How have poets become popular in China since the 1970s? Did they get noticed on the basis of radical expression, or courageous language, or good craftsmanship?

Song Lin:

From the late 1970s to the mid-1980s, the Misty poets represented by Bei Dao became popular mainly due to a conceptual change. Since the mid-1980s, the "third generation" poets became prominent due to their concern with language per se. While critics remarked upon various declarations to "change the language," true language revolutions occurred quietly. In the 1990s, some poets proposed "personal writing," "middle-aged writing," etc. The most controversial was "intellectual writing," which was confronted with "plain speech writing" and the compromised "third road writing."

Since the beginning of this century, "local writing" and "grass-roots writing" have gained more attention. Perhaps it's due to the lack of independent thinking that people always look for "concepts" rather than (responding directly to) the art of poetry itself.

Do anthologies in China effectively sort out and identify important poets? What are the most important anthologies since the 1970s, and who was omitted from those anthologies? Are there any poets who have gone unnoticed but you think deserve more attention?

Song Lin:

In every age there are certain poets who are sheltered while other poets are famous. One has to wait until censorship is lifted. The next generation can choose who they think are most noteworthy. Du Fu's contemporaries did not realize his value. There is perhaps no such thing as "commonly agreed-upon anthologies" in contemporary China, therefore the omission (of certain poets) has become a typical phenomenon.

Who are the major poetry critics in China? Have they gained authority or trust? How?

Song Lin:
The majority of scholars engaged in poetry criticism are within universities and research institutions. They write due to the requirements of their profession and they seem to favor historical periods rather than the current time. The chaos in poetry criticism is even more severe than the chaos in poetry. (We should not blame the critics for the chaos in the poetry field.)

And yet after all, having one or two qualified, confident critics to stimulate your writing is more than enough.

However, despite the fact that current poetry criticism doesn't have much positive influence, I tend to trust critics such as Tang Xiaodu, Chen Chao, Geng Zhanchun, and Jiang Ruoshui.

But the important theoretical issues have been raised by poets and poet-critics.

You write critical essays, too. How do you separate the two roles of poet and critic? Does critical writing affect your creative writing, and if yes, in what ways?

Song Lin:
Poets intervening with poetry criticism is a last resort, but also naturally predicted by poetry writing itself. Of course creative writing comes first.

It would be a problem if the overall quality of criticism in a certain age were a greater achievement than the poetry. Personally, I find that writing critical essays does not interfere with my creative writing; beyond poetry writing, it's an extra joy.

HU XUDONG

Was there anything extraordinary in your childhood that affected your writing later on?

Hu Xudong:
I spent my first seven years in a rural village in Chongqing. The vulgar slang, the swelling curiosity about new things, and the explosive joyfulness of my earlier years in the countryside came

surprisingly into my poetry writing later. I often feel that writing poetry in a big city like Beijing is a way of compensating for leaving the village too early, which took the joy from my soul.

What books "enlightened" you in earlier years, and in what ways?

Hu Xudong:

In my high school days, I was a delinquent juvenile hanging out with a gang. They stole four sacks of books from the library and gave me two sacks. Holy God, I started reading Gabriel Garcia Marquez, Mario Vargos Llosa, Joseph Heller, Yasunari Kawabata, Franz Kafka, Karel Capek, and so on. I was poisoned immediately! My literary taste was formed by those stolen books. It was the secret reading that made me believe: good literature has great mystery; reading literature is like engaging in underground activities.

How and when did you start writing poetry?

Hu Xudong:

I was doing traditional Chinese painting and became a minor celebrity. At a solo exhibition, out of a sense of the traditional format, I thought I should write some classical poetry to go with the paintings and make them look more complete. So I began to do the eighteen rhymes, and all sorts of classical things. But then I realized it didn't go along with the two sacks of (modern) books I had read. As my painting career ended, so did my fake classical poetry writing.

I didn't start writing the "New Poetry" until 1992 when I entered Beijing University. I joined the May Fourth Literary Club on the campus without knowing why. Writing poetry was like hanging out with a gang in high school, a sort of mysterious and exciting thing.

What's a good poem to you? Whose poetry is "good" or which poets do you like the most?

Hu Xudong:

The most fascinating thing about poetry is that it refuses to provide a blueprint for the ideal, and it constantly troubles you, so I have never been able to reach the "goal." I like Portuguese poet Fernando Pessoa and Brazilian poet Joao Cabral de Melo Neto. The former let me see that however broken inside, heart and body, one can still build a huge empire of poetry from the broken pieces. The latter made me realize that a poet can work like an engineer, making the most dazzling thing in calmness.

How do you evaluate the occurrence of new poetry? How do you judge the current Chinese poetry?

Hu Xudong:
I'm not able to evaluate the origin of the new poetry. As a member of a younger generation, I can only accept the self-striving, poor origin of this poetry, which stood outside the enormous wealth of Chinese traditional poetry and tried so hard to sell itself.

I like the vitality of contemporary Chinese poetry, but I don't quite like the cultural ecological symptoms.

Generally speaking, there's a gigantic ancient poetry tradition. There's Mao-era poetry (especially Mao's own poetry); there's the Enlightenment mission of the Misty poetry in the late 1970s; there's the country-wide rhapsody of the 1980s; there's the 1990s poetry that's too solemn and "value"-oriented; and there's the twenty-first–century poetry that's too seriously defending "morality."

All of these add a lot of unnecessary aura — this illusory aura interferes with a normal understanding of poetry as a craft.

What do you think of poetry translation in China, the selection and the quality? Whose work have you translated?

Hu Xudong:
I very much agree with what the American poet and translator Kenneth Rexroth said: translation "is the best way to keep your tools sharp until the great job, the great moment, comes along." I translate, and "translation saves you from your contemporaries." Through your own translation and reading, you change your literary kinship and your tradition.

I gained a basic understanding of modern poetry from reading Western poetry in translation, but now in retrospect I find that many of those translations were of poor quality. I myself have translated a few poems by Ted Hughes, Seamus Heaney, and Derek Walcott. I did some by Yehuda Amichai and Tomaž Šalamun, based on English translations. Then directly from the Portuguese I translated Fernando Pessoa out of momentary interest.

I also enjoy critical essays written by poets. My most enjoyable translation has to be translating Paul Muldoon's essays. His close reading of Fernando Pessoa's poetry is comparable to detective stories, with so much complexity.

What do you think of Chinese poetry being translated into English or other languages?

Hu Xudong:
The anthologies of contemporary Chinese poetry in English translation that I have seen are usually promoted by the numbers of poets that each has included (as if "the more the better"), with each poet "represented" by just a few poems. It's a very persuasive way to answer the question, "Are there any poets in contemporary China?" — but this fails to answer who they are, how good they are, and who all the good poets out there are.

I don't think it's necessary to put so many names in an anthology to represent a nation or a country. There was a slim anthology published in Spain in 2009 entitled *La Niebla de Nuestra Edad* (*The Fog of Our Age: Ten Contemporary Chinese Poets*). I think it's very good. It has selected some low-key but cool poets.

I don't think we should worry too much about "mis-translating" or "lost in translation." Sometimes misreading in translation may bring an unexpected effect. I can cite two examples here. A Taiwanese American translated my "cigarettes of Yellow Fruit brand" into "a train carrying a large waterfall." Fantastic image! Much better than my original. A Spanish poet translated my "big tongue rain" (a joke about the Shandong dialect) as "It was raining many big tongues." Compared to my original line, the translation is much more surreal!

LÜ YUE

As an engaged poet and senior editor of the "New Beijing" newspaper with a poetry column, what have you observed in current poetry writing? What are poets concerned with nowadays?

Lü Yue:

From what I've seen, many poets are more concerned with social problems than language or imagination or aesthetics, which translates into writing about personal experience in the society. The realist tradition is very strong in Chinese literature and poetry, and our country is facing many problems, but I don't deny individual differences, as other poets and writers have their own concerns.

What do you see as the core issues in Chinese contemporary poetry?

Lü Yue:

Everything comes down to humanity. From the 1960s to the '70s there was underground poetry. From the '70s to the '80s there was Misty poetry, which represented a social "awakening." In the late 1980s, the "third generation" came along, raising the slogan that "poetry ends with language" and emphasizing language experimentation, independent from ideological concerns. After 1989 major changes took place — there was disappointment, isolation, alienation, and a switch of attention to consumer society. Since the beginning of the new century, with the rise of the Internet and public involvement in political and cultural issues, poetry writing is "liberated" and individualized.

What do you see is the major problem?

Lü Yue:

Lack of value standards, uncertainties of aesthetics, and prevailing nihilism lead to "incompleteness" of poetry, in terms of forms and meanings.

How about poetry criticism? What role does it play?

Lü Yue:

In classical Chinese literature, theory and practice went hand in hand; poetry criticism set the standard for what's "good" and established the canon. In modern and contemporary China, criticism has a very limited role. Poetry reviewing is weak.

How is poetry doing overall?

Lü Yue:

From the 1970s to the 1980s, poets were spokesmen of a whole generation. Poetry was at the core of the society. In current China, fiction writing is popular, as fiction is in the center of consumerism, while poetry is becoming marginalized, like everywhere else in the world.

FENG YAN

Your poetry is different from that of most women poets writing in China — unsentimental, impersonal, unemotional, and non-physical. How and when did you start writing poetry?

Feng Yan:

My parents were divorced and lived apart, so I moved around from my early years on, and I have never been to college. But I've read extensively, especially Western literature and philosophy, such as the work of Schopenhauer, Nietzsche, Kierkegaard, Berdyaev, Bakhtin, Kafka, Camus, Dostoevsky, Kurt Vonnegut, etc., etc.

I started writing poetry when I was reading Shelley, Byron, and Lermontov, and later I was influenced by Hölderlin.

I'm particularly fond of Susan Langer's books. I enjoy reading Wittgenstein most. My writing is a little philosophical, because what we as women poets lack most is logical thinking. Reading helps me overcome my shortcomings.

I'll tell you who I like: Borges, Trakl, Hölderlin, Celan, Milosz, Zagajewski, Mark Strand, and so on. I like the deep thinking and intensity in their work. I hope to have their strength.

What do you try to achieve in poetry?

Feng Yan:

I try to create a new rhythm in poetry, a linguistic sharpness or power with penetrating emotion, a kind of poetry that professional poets would fall in love with, when they read.

In recent years I have written some long poems and experimented with different approaches.

To me, writing poetry is to find light in words, the light that we've lost in life.

Do you exchange ideas with other poets?

Feng Yan:
I have a few friends in Harbin, such as Zhang Shuguang, and Sang Ke. There are other people I've met during poetry festivals, but we don't talk about poetry.

How do you look at poetry circles in China?

Feng Yan:
Writing is personal, but a good writing circle will push you forward. So I think it's meaningful but difficult to form a circle, because it takes a leader, and you have to find a style that surpasses other people. It takes talent, artistic creativity, and friendship.

We don't have great thinkers. We don't have readers for poetry either.

XIAO KAIYU

When did you start writing poetry and why? Is there anything peculiar about your writing?

Xiao Kaiyu:
I began to write poetry at age twenty-six. This was a calm decision. I felt it was my cup of tea and I've never stopped. Being an empiricist, I rely on my experience, but with a different focus during each phase of time. I don't write beyond my experience. I'm a little aesthetic, but also a bit critical, and I always attempt to accommodate both.

What's a "good" poem to you?

Xiao Kaiyu:
"Readable" is okay. If I have to avoid someone, then he's really good.

What do you mean by "avoid"?

Xiao Kaiyu:
If a poet has experimented with something to the last possible out-

come and that style becomes his brand, then I should stay away from him.

What do you think of poetry movements or poetry circles in China? Have you participated in any debates about poetics?

Xiao Kaiyu:
I'm not concerned about that; I've never been part of any group or circle, and never been in any debate. I have my three self-restraints: anti-totalitarian, neo-idealism, and contemporary poetry.

How do you define each?

Xiao Kaiyu:
The first is self-explanatory. The second one is a refined principle formed out of good will — a new idealism, not materialism, nor the old German idealism. Thirdly, I don't write modern poetry. Adorno's argument ended the validity of modernism: "to write a poem after Auschwitz is barbaric ..." I only consider the significance of poetry within contemporary art and contemporary thought.

What is "contemporary" to you?

Xiao Kaiyu:
It's my bias that I don't write within the coordinates of modernity. The meaning of poetry generates from within the framework of contemporary schools of thoughts and contemporary art theories.

Many contemporary Chinese poets start with modern poetry; some are still very "modern," and they talk about "modernity" every day. How come you resist modernity?

Xiao Kaiyu:
I'm an ordinary person from a small place. I see the world only from my own experience. If modern poetry contradicts my literary awareness, I will only be faithful to my own consciousness.

What do you think of Chinese New Poetry? And what do you think of its current status?

Xiao Kaiyu:
New Poetry started from self-renewal, and it's been trying very hard. At the current time it's doing better than ever.

Have you ever been influenced by the Misty poetry?

Xiao Kaiyu:
Up until today I haven't read Misty poetry. I respect its history, but I don't read it.

How do you see Chinese poetry in the 1990s?

Xiao Kaiyu: The focus in the 1990s was to increase the awareness of "completeness" in the texts. If you didn't go through the 1990s in China as a Chinese poet, your work will be either fragmented or obsolete.

There is an opinion that you introduced "narrative" writing into Chinese poetry in the 1990s. What would you say about it?

Xiao Kaiyu:
Narrative writing means to use prose syntax — that is, declarative sentences — so you will have to write with a certain contemporary practical experience. This is not a new practice. In the history of Chinese literature, every innovation movement was a renaissance. Using prose syntactics is an effective way to touch the ground of raw reality. I said that. But the followers have their own pursuits, resulting in more and more vulgar and trivial writing. I'm not responsible for that.

Your independent magazine "The Nineties" was very influential in the 1990s, wasn't it?

Xiao Kaiyu:
It was a small privately printed journal, so how could it be influential? It published some readable poems. All I remember was that it published Zhang Shuguang's earlier work. Other work could have been published anywhere else.

ZHANG SHUGUANG

Were there any childhood experiences that affected your writing?

Zhang Shuguang:
Illness and death. I wrote about them in my poems.

I caught tuberculosis at age three, which was not curable in those days in China.

My younger sister died of illness at seven months. She simply disappeared.

Were there any books that influenced you?

Zhang Shuguang:
All the books that I could get hold of. I was hungry for knowledge. Up to this day I still read everything by first-rate writers, and by writers of third and fourth and fifth rate, too.

Pushkin influenced me most. Lu Xun, too. In my college days, my favorite authors were Kafka, Proust, Beckett, and Borges. Later on, Wittgenstein and Derrida. More recently (Slovenian philosopher) Slavoj Žižek. But most of all, Zen.

Why do you write poetry?

Zhang Shuguang:
Writing poetry is very natural for me. I was very lyrical when I was under the influence of Pushkin. Later on when I was exposed to modernism, I began to dilute the lyrical yearning and started writing narrative poetry. Beginning in the 1990s I became more conscious of making changes.

How do you find and maintain your own voice?

Zhang Shuguang:
I'd like to borrow Eliot's words: a second-rate writer is inevitably reluctant to participate in any common action because his main task is to maintain his own distinctive trivial features. Something like that. I'm a third-, fourth-, fifth-, sixth-, seventh-, eighth-, and ninth-rate writer, but still I will not act like what T. S. Eliot called a second-rate writer. If you can lose your voice so easily, let it go.

What do you think of the poetry movements or schools or circles in China?

Zhang Shuguang:
They can be very meaningful and important. But there have been none in China — nothing significant. Symbolists and modernists made a tremendous achievement. We have done nothing like that yet.

Editor's Surveys: Favorite Lists

Who do you think are the ten most interesting poets in contemporary China?

Bai Hua:
Bian Zhilin, for his craftsmanship; Bei Dao, who influenced me most; Zhang Zao, my most precious poet friend, who inspired me frequently; and Lu Yimin, the most gifted female poet in the 1980s.

Zhang Shuguang:
The question is how you define "interesting." Do you mean "playfulness," as in Chen Danqing's comment on Lu Xun? Or juvenile fun, like in (the physicist) Feynman's work? Anyway, I don't think we have many interesting poets in contemporary China. We have good craftsmen, serious poets, and ambitious poets, but very few interesting poets.

Sun Wenbo:
It's not an easy thing to name only ten poets, so I will exclude those who have already been introduced to Western countries. I believe the following ten poets have played a major part in the development of contemporary Chinese poetry: Sun Wenbo, Zang Di, Qing Ping, Zhang Shuguang, Jiang Tao, Jiang Hao, Xiao Kaiyu, Ya Shi, Xi Du, and Ming Di. Their work has fundamentally changed Chinese poetry since 1990, shifting poetry more toward social life. They have elevated the overall quality of contemporary poetry in China by emphasizing concrete and precise diction.

Song Lin:
Duo Duo, for the tension in his language and his forceful style. Xi Chuan, for the composite candor of his texts. Wang Jiaxin, for his weighty reflective thinking and clumsiness. Bai Hua, for his stylish language and his way of confronting history with poetry. Yu Jian, for being direct, profound, with a sense of directions. Zhai Yongming, for her intrinsic drama and feminist perspective. Lü De'an, for plain but textured language, and for the fable style. Chen Dongdong, for brightness and musicality, with moderate irony. Huang Canran, for his patient, impersonal style and

religious sense. And Ouyang Jianghe, for eloquence, gorgeous with complex details.

Xiao Kaiyu:

I never recommend poets or poems because I don't read poets or poems recommended by other people.

Translators should work harder, and not focus on famous but worthless poets, so readers from other countries could learn more about Chinese poetry. On the other hand, I don't think we have anything worth their attention right now.

Zang Di:

Wang Ao's fresh language has revitalized Chinese. Qing Ping has a very peculiar linguistic sense. Jiang Hao has explored the potentials of Chinese as a language for poetry. Ya Shi has a rare sense of contemporariness. Huang Canran hides himself and seeks the honesty of language. Jiang Tao has the most trenchant and most merciful irony. Hu Xudong has an unlimited appetite for contemporary rhythms.

Ya Shi:

From 1990 to the present, I personally find that the most interesting contemporary writers who are actively engaged in poetry include Sun Wenbo, Zhang Shuguang, Zang Di, Jiang Tao, Hu Xudong, Jiang Hao, Yu Xiang, Lei Pingyang, Chen Xianfa, and Yu Nu. My considerations are based on whether I can find different qualities in their work, different from my own. For instance, Sun Wenbo's poetry may look simple but carries hidden power and intelligence. Jiang Tao's work may appear casual but has deep sensitivity.

Jiang Tao:

Duo Duo, Bai Hua, Xiao Kaiyu, Zang Di, Zhang Zao, Chen Dongdong, and Ouyang Jianghe. I highly regard their work and I think they each have separately made contributions in exploring the possibilities of Chinese poetry.

Jiang Hao:

Every ten years there have been changes in contemporary Chinese poetry. From the 1990s to the end of last century, the poets who were worth reading include Xi Chuan, Ouyang Jianghe, Zhang Zao, and Zhang Shuguang. Since the beginning of the new century, the most innovative, original, and pioneering poets have been Xiao Kaiyu, Zang Di, Sun Wenbo, Han Bo, Jiang Tao, Hu Xudong, and myself, Jiang Hao.

Lü Yue:
Hu Kuan, an avant-garde poet who started writing poetry in the 1970s. The Collected Poems of Hu Kuan was published posthumously by his friends in 1996, and he was then "rediscovered" by poetry critics.

Other important poets are Yu Jian, Wang Xiaoni, Li Yawei, Zheng Danyi, Yang Jian, Song Xiaoxian, and Wu Ang.

Hu Xudong:
In terms of having unique styles and expanding the boundaries of Chinese contemporary poetry writing: Xi Chuan, Zang Di, Xiao Kaiyu, Zhang Zao, Zhai Yongming, Jiang Tao, Jiang Hao, Ma Yan, Wang Ao, and Han Bo.

Jiang Li:
I have two categories. First, nine poets that I have looked forward to reading: Ouyang Jianghe, Zhang Shuguang, Yu Jian, Sun Wenbo, Xiao Kaiyu, Zang Di, Huang Canran, Ye Hui, and Zhu Yongliang; they have demonstrated a sustained seriousness in poetry writing with distinctive styles — very enlightening. Secondly, nine poets I personally find interesting: Mang Ke, Hai Po, Mo Mo, Pan Wei, Yang Li, Shen Haobo, Li Yawei, Yi Sha, and Cai Tianxin; they are interesting in different ways — each of them has a personality.

Which ten Chinese poets (from ancient times to the present) have influenced you most?

Bai Hua:
Too many to list. I will just mention two: Wu Wenying (c. 1200–c. 1260) and Huang Tingjian (1045–1105).

Zhang Shuguang:
When I was young I used to like Li Bai, Du Fu, Su Shi, and Wang Wei, and so forth. Later I preferred Tao Yuanming and the (anonymous) authors of "Nineteen Ancient Poems." As for contemporary

poets, I've read some and some of them are my good friends, but it's hard to pinpoint a specific impact from them.

Sun Wenbo:
The following ancient Chinese poets have influenced me: Du Fu, Tao Yuanming, Su Dongpo, Xin Qiji, Cao Cao, Cao Zhi, Shen Yue, Xiao Gang, and Xiao Yi, and anonymous authors of the "Nineteen Ancient Poems." Western readers must read them if they want to know about Chinese classical poetry because these are the most outstanding ones, in my opinion.

Song Lin:
Qu Yuan, Tao Qian, Li Bai, Du Fu, Li Shangyin, Wang Wei, Su Shi, Lu Xun (1881–1936), Bian Zhilin (1910–2000), and Bei Dao.

Zang Di:
Wang Wei, Su Dongpo (Su Shi), Du Fu, Li Shangyin, Li Bai, Tao Yuanming, Mu Dan (1918–1977), Wang Ao (1976–), Qing Ping (1962–), and Bian Zhilin (1910–2000).

Ya Shi:
Ancient poets Chen Zi-ang, Li Bai, Du Fu, Huang Shan-gu, and Wang Wei and contemporary poet Bai Hua have influenced my earlier writing.

Jiang Tao:
Classical poet Du Fu; modern poets Feng Zhi and Mu Dan; contemporary poets Hai Zi, Xi Chuan, Zang Di, Ouyang Jianghe, and Xiao Kaiyu.

Jiang Hao:
I would list classical poets only: Qu Yuan, Xie Lingyun, Li Bai, Du Fu, Li Shangyin, Bai Juyi, Su Dongpo, Wang Wei, Lu You, and Xin Qiji.

Lü Yue:
From the ancient time: the *Book of Songs,* the Han Folk Songs, Li Bai, Du Fu, and Su Shi. Modern poets: Fei Ming, Bian Zhilin, Mu Dan. And contemporary poets: Bei Dao and Zhai Yongming.

Hu Xudong:
Classical poets: Ruan Ji and Li Bai. Modern poets: Bian Zhilin and Fei Ming. And contemporary poets: Duo Duo, Bai Hua, Xiao Kaiyu, Zhang Zao, Xi Chuan, and Zang Di.

Jiang Li:
Classical poets: Qu Yuan, the anonymous authors of the "Nineteen Ancient Poems," Tao Yuanming, Xie Lingyun, Wang Wei, Meng Haoran, Li Bai, Du Fu, Bai Juyi, and Su Dongpo. Contemporary poets: Zhang Shuguang, Ye Hui, Sun Wenbo, Zang Di, Xiao Kaiyu, Lü De'an, Huang Canran, Pan Wei, Sang Ke, and Cai Tianxin.

Which Western poets have been most influential on contemporary Chinese poetry?

Bai Hua:
Too many to count.

Zhang Shuguang:
Chinese poets gain knowledge of foreign poets mostly through translation, not from (free) personal choice. So it all depends on the perspectives of the translators. This reflects how important translation is. First we had T. S. Eliot and Rilke, then we had Milosz and Brodsky. By the late 1990s, more poets were introduced into China and we had more choices to make. Many poets promote Cavafy, but few seem to have learned his essence.

Sun Wenbo:
Western literature from ancient Greece down to the present has had a significant impact on Chinese literature and poetry. Since the modernist movement was introduced into China, the following poets have had the greatest influence on Chinese poets: Yeats, Pound, Eliot, Wallace Stevens, Ashbery, and Ginsberg; French poets Baudelaire, Mallarme, Rimbaud, Valery, and the surrealists; German poets Rilke, Trakl, and Celan; and the Russian or Eastern European poets Mandelstam, Pasternak, Akhmatova, Milosz, Zbigniew Herbert, and Brodsky. Foremost, they changed our concept of what poetry is, so that we had a new starting point in re-understanding the traditional Chinese poetry and in building

new forms. This meant revolutionary change in the language. For example, Pound helped us get rid of what must be abandoned; Eliot helped us build an entirely new relationship with poetry and traditions.

Song Lin:
Dante, Baudelaire, Hölderlin, Whitman, Pound, Yeats, Eliot, Rilke, Valery, Frost, Borges, Wallace Stevens, Lorca, Mandelstam, Tsvetaeva, Pasternak, Celan, Milosz, Brodsky, Cavafy, Tranströmer, Heaney.

Xiao Kaiyu:
I can tell you who I'm reading right now: new and collected poems of George Szirtes.

Zang Di:
Eliot, Rilke, Pound, Yeats, Wallace Stevens, Ginsberg, Valery, Montale, Brodsky, Milosz, Ted Hughes, Plath, and Elizabeth Bishop have had significant impact on Chinese contemporary poetry. For instance, Eliot awakened the modern consciousness in Chinese poets and an awareness of how to deal with the relationship between traditions and individual talents. Rilke led contemporary Chinese poets into overcoming the sentimentalism of earlier Chinese free verse poetry — a variant of romanticism. Pound encouraged our aspirations for language innovations. Yeats, with his efforts in adopting "masks" and a symbolic "self," helped us distance our writing from the state literature. Wallace Stevens demonstrated the role of imagination in writing.

Ya Shi:
In the evolving phases of Chinese New Poetry, Eliot, Auden, Rilke, Valery, and Baudelaire have left clear marks. Their concepts of poetry and their works are part of the formation of Chinese modern poetry. Auden came to China and wrote about Chinese current affairs then, which might be one of the reasons he influenced us. Since the late 1980s, Chinese poetry has "encountered" Wallace Stevens, Brodsky, Heaney, Milosz, and Zagajewski for various poetic reasons. To answer this question requires historical insight and detailed case studies. Every poet would have a different answer, and the map is tinted by personal growth.

Jiang Tao:
Eliot, Brodsky, Rilke, Borges, Auden, Robert Lowell, Larkin, and Ashbery. Their influences are in two main areas, first in establishing a certain poetic consciousness, and secondly in developing poetic styles.

Jiang Hao:
Mallarme and Valery freed Chinese poets from ideological concerns. Rilke is somehow in resonance with ancient Chinese poetics. Eliot's poetry and essays have had decisive influence on contemporary Chinese poetry and poetry criticism — no other Western poet has been more influential than him. Pound, Milosz, Brodsky, Stevens, Frost, and Ashbery have each affected certain aspects of Chinese poetry. Frost reminds us of our beloved classical poet Tao Yuanming. Ashbery's poetry leads us to a more conceptualized art, which is absent in Chinese tradition.

Lü Yue:
Baudelaire: completely new, startling. Whitman: free form and free spirit. Rilke: clear language and perfection in craftsmanship. Allen Ginsberg: critical and destructive, with a strong auditory effect.

Hu Xudong:
Baudelaire, Rimbaud, Mallarmé, Valery, and the surrealist poets in the French tradition influenced Chinese poetry in the 1930s and 1940s as well as 1980s, which brought about a basic awareness of modern poetry.

Yeats, Pound, Eliot, Wallace Stevens, and Auden in the English tradition have each had influence upon Chinese poets, in different ways and at different times, in terms of intellectual thinking and overall creativity.

Russian poets Akhmatova, Tsvetaeva, and Mandelstam have strengthened the lyrical expressions in Chinese poetry. Trakl, Rilke, and Celan in the German tradition enriched the "depth" of Chinese poetry. Lorca and Neruda and other Spanish voices have affected the emotional presentation of Chinese poetry.

Allen Ginsberg brought a rebellious impulse in the 1980s. Sylvia Plath and other "confessional" poets injected a strong shot into Chinese women's poetry in the 1980s.

Heaney, Milosz, Paz, and Walcott have helped Chinese poets in re-adjusting the relationship between reality and imagination, history and writing ethics, modernism and contemporary writing.

Since 2000, Western poetry has rarely had a "global" impact on Chinese contemporary writing. Its penetration into the discourse of Chinese poetry is mostly local and even personal, sometimes in an extremely private way. For instance, some Eastern European poets, such as Zbigniew Herbert, Zagajewski, and Tomaž Šalamun, have aroused great attention. Some American poets who did not initially leave big impressions or had only slight popularity are now becoming strong inspirations: Hart Crane, Frank O'Hara, Bishop, and Ashbery. Similarly with the "forgotten" non-English poets: Cavafy, Machado, Vallejo, and Yehuda Amichai. They have attracted more interest as more translations have appeared. Fernando Pessoa has also become a personal source of inspiration for some Chinese poets.

Jiang Li:

The following poets have had a strong impact on Chinese poetry since the 1980s: Whitman, Hölderlin, Baudelaire, Rimbaud, Pound, Yeats, Frost, Wallace Stevens, Eliot, Rilke, Lorca, Akhmatova, Mandelstam, Cavafy, Saint-John Perse, Auden, Borges, Pessoa, Heaney, Brodsky, Milosz, and Yannis Ritsos. Chinese "New Poetry" experienced a rupture in the 1950s and regained interest in Western literature in the 1970s. Within thirty years of time, Chinese poets absorbed the hundred-year history of Western modern poetry. The main impact of this was on the writing of poetry, but the influence went beyond poetry. Bei Dao's generation was influenced by symbolic poetry. The "third generation" was more influenced by post–World War I poetry, especially Beat poetry. Currently, Chinese classical poetry is becoming a vital source of inspiration for us. This Chinese-Western fusion will be an important part of new Chinese poetry in the years to come.

Which Asian poets have been most influential on contemporary Chinese poets?

Bai Hua:
Japanese writer Sei Shōnagon with her work "The Pillow Book" has influenced me since 1990, and even more so now.

Zhang Shuguang:
I think the real influence, if any, came from Rabindranath Tagore — but whether that influence has been good or bad, it's still hard to say. It's difficult to pinpoint other Asian poets.

Sun Wenbo:
Overall, Asian poetry hasn't had a great impact on Chinese contemporary poetry. Tagore may have had some influence, but due to the inadequate translations, he wasn't presented as one of the greatest thinkers in Asia, and therefore he had very limited influence on contemporary Chinese poets. The *Rubáiyát* of the Persian Omar Khayyám has had a certain influence on some Chinese poets' writing.

Song Lin:
Tagore, Khayyám, Matsuo Basho, Kahlil Gibran.

Zang Di:
It's hard to pinpoint individual influences from Asian poets. Japanese poetry played a role in shaping Chinese New Poetry, but due to the Sino-Japanese War, the effect easily slipped into a question of "politically correct or not." Tagore influenced Chinese poetry earlier on, but quickly this influence was distorted into sentimental cliché. Classical Indian poetry had a significant impact on some Chinese poets, such as Hai Zi in the 1980s. Chinese poets are now becoming more interested in poetry in India, Iran, and Palestine.

Ya Shi:
I can't think of Asian poets that have strong influence on our contemporary poetry.

Jiang Tao:
Influence from Asian poetry is relatively smaller than the influence of Western literature. This is a problem of acceptance and perspectives, since the 1980s. We've looked more to Europe and the United States, lacking an interest in the real diversities of "World Literature."

Jiang Hao:
None.

Lü Yue:
Tagore, since the 1920s. Very few Asian poets have been introduced into China through the 1980s. Since the 1990s, Tanikawa Shuntaro has been translated, Yehuda Amichai from Israel has been translated, and Syrian Arabic poet Adonis has gained much attention.

Hu Xudong:
Japanese poet Tanikawa Shuntaro has been translated into Chinese, but it's difficult to judge if there has been any impact of his work on Chinese poets. Some of the Chinese poets have turned to poetry in the Mideast, West Asia, and South Asia to refresh their inspiration, but it's difficult to make any conclusion as to whether there has been any influence from there.

Jiang Li:
Tagore for a while, but that didn't last long.

Which ten living poets from all other countries (including younger poets and newer voices) are your favorites?

Bai Hua:
Thomas Tranströmer, Herta Muller, Paul Muldoon, and Jan Wagner.

Zhang Shuguang:
Most of my favorite poets are dead. I haven't read enough younger poets, or there haven't been many introduced to China. I would just name Ashbery, Zagajewski, Heaney, and the earlier Li-Young Lee. In poetry reading I prefer younger poets, not because they are better but because they have something new to attract me.

Sun Wenbo:
Walcott, Heaney, and Zagajewski. They are not necessarily my favorites, but I read them to learn what's going on out there. The young poets you translated last year give me a deep impression, and I see great potential in their work.

Song Lin:
Heaney, Tranströmer, and Zagajewski.

Xiao Kaiyu:
There are many good poets, poets from Ireland, poets from Hungary, and so on.

Zang Di:
Simon Armitage, Paul Muldoon, Seamus Heaney, Durs Grünbein, Hans Magnus Enzensberger, Charles Wright, Jorie Graham, Louise Glück, and Aleš Šteger.

Ya Shi:
Currently I like John Ashbery, who is very sophisticated, and Seamus Heaney, who is clear and solid without lacking linguistic complexity. Of the younger poets, the one you've translated appeals to me strongly. I'm drawn to the sense of pain and joy of language in his poetry and the way Russian tradition expands in his work.

Jiang Tao:
I have read some contemporary poets who are active in other countries, but honestly I haven't done enough careful evaluation and comparison.

Jiang Hao:
John Ashbery, Mark Strand, W. S. Merwin, Charles Wright, and Robert Bly.

Lü Yue:
Marin Sorescu from Romania, Wislawa Szymborska from Poland, Ana Blandiana from Romania, Ivan Zhdanov from Russia, Adonis from Syria, Adam Zagajewski from Poland, Tomas Venclova from Lithuania, Tanigawa Shuntaro from Japan, and that young Russian-American poet you translated.

Hu Xudong:
Among the living international poets, I have been paying most attention to Heaney, Walcott, and Tranströmer, and in recent years to Juan Gelman (Argentina), Jose Emilio Pacheco (Mexico), Ferreira Gullar (Brazil), Tomaž Šalamun (Slovenia), and Robert Hass and Forrest Gander (U.S.). As for younger poets, I find the following poets interesting: Scottish poet W. N. Herbert, and Slovenian poet Aleš Šteger, Macedonian poet Nikola Madzirov, and Croatian poet Marko Pogacar.

Jiang Li:
Derek Walcott, John Ashbery, Zbigniew Herbert, W. S. Merwin, Adam Zagajewski, Tomas Tranströmer, Robert Bly, Louise Glück, and Charles Simic.

Editor's note: The "favorite Western poets" listed here reflect what has been translated into Chinese so far, and the opinions given only represent the poets interviewed.

About the Editor and Translators

Ming Di, editor (明迪, pen name of Mindy Zhang) was born and grew up in China. She did graduate studies in linguistics at Boston University before moving to California, where she translates poetry and literary essays from both English and Chinese, with two volumes published and three forthcoming. Author of six collections of original poetry in Chinese and one in English translation, *River Merchant's Wife* (Marick Press, 2012), she also edits *Poetry East West*, a bilingual literary journal published in Los Angeles and Beijing.

Nick Admussen (安敏轩) is an assistant professor of Chinese at Widener University in Chester, Pennsylvania. His translations have appeared in *Renditions* and *Cha Magazine;* his original poetry has appeared in *Boston Review, Fence,* and *The Kenyon Review Online,* as well as in the chapbook *Movie Plots* (Epiphany Editions, 2010). He is currently researching the prose poetry of Lu Xun and translating Ya Shi's *Qingcheng Poems.*

Neil Aitken (艾仁才) is the author of *The Lost Country of Sight* (winner of the 2007 Philip Levine Prize for Poetry; Anhinga Press, 2008), the founding editor of *Boxcar Poetry Review,* and a contributing editor for *Poetry East West.* A Canadian of Chinese and Scottish descent, he presently lives in Los Angeles, where he is completing a PhD in literature and creative writing at the University of Southern California.

Tony Barnstone holds an endowed chair in English at Whittier College and is author of twelve books, including *Tongue of War: From Pearl Harbor to Nagasaki,* winner of the John Ciardi Prize in Poetry (BKMK Press, 2009) and *The Golem of Los Angeles,* winner of the Benjamin Saltman Award in Poetry (Red Hen Press, 2007). Dr. Barnstone is a distinguished translator of Chinese poetry, with multiple volumes in print, and he is an editor of three previous anthologies, *Out of the Howling Storm: The New Chinese Poetry* (Wesleyan University Press, 1993) and *The Anchor Book of Chinese Poetry* (Anchor, 2005), and *Chinese Erotic Poems* (Everyman, 2007).

KATIE FARRIS is the author of *BOYSGIRLS* (Marick Press, 2011) and co-translator of Polina Barskova's *This Lamentable City* (Tupelo Press, 2010). Her work has appeared in *Virginia Quarterly Review, The Literary Review, Verse, The Mid-American Review,* and other journals. She is an assistant professor of English and comparative literature at San Diego State University.

ELEANOR GOODMAN (顾爱玲) writes poetry, fiction, and criticism, and she translates from Chinese. Her work has appeared in journals such as *Pathlight, PN Review, Los Angeles Review, Chutzpah, Pleiades, The Guardian,* and *Cha,* and on the *Best American Poetry* website. She is a research associate at the Fairbank Center for Chinese Studies at Harvard University.

KERRY SHAWN KEYS received the Robert H. Winner Memorial Award from the Poetry Society of America in 1992 and the Translation Laureate Award from the Lithuanian Writers Union in 2003. In 2011, two new books of his translations from Lithuanian were published: *Bootleg Copy,* poems of Laurynas Katkus (Virtual Artists Collective) and *Still Life,* poems of Sonata Paliulyte (co-translated with Irena Praitis; Calder Wood Press).

JENNIFER KRONOVET is the author of the poetry collection *Awayward* (BOA Editions, 2009) and a founding editor of *Circumference,* the journal of poetry in translation. Born and raised in New York City, she has also lived in Beijing, Chicago, and St. Louis.

DIAN LI (李点) holds a PhD in Asian Languages and Cultures from the University of Michigan–Ann Arbor. He is now an associate professor and associate head in the Department of East Asian Studies, University of Arizona–Tucson. He has published more than fifty essays, reviews, and translations in the fields of literary theory, modern Chinese poetry, and film studies, including a monograph on Chinese poet Bei Dao.

CHRISTOPHER LUPKE (陆敬思) is associate professor of Chinese language and culture at Washington State University, where he serves as coordinator of Asian languages. His area of specialization is modern and contemporary Chinese literature and culture, and he has published books on the Chinese concept of "ming" (fate, destiny, life) and on contemporary Chinese poetry. His translations have appeared in journals such as *Chinese PEN, Taiwan Literature, Five Points, Cha,* and *Free Verse.*

CODY REESE was born in Portland, Oregon, and is currently a student at Whittier College in Los Angeles, where he is finishing his degree in English and creative writing. He also studies music and philosophy, as a double minor. He has been published in his college's journal, *The Literary Review.*

ELIZABETH REITZELL is a creative writing and philosophy double major at Whittier College. For her poem "Someone's Daughter," she was awarded a 2012 Honorable Mention in her college's journal, *The Literary Review;* in 2012 she received the Keck Fellowship, which funded a month-long monastic Buddhist retreat in Taiwan.

JONATHAN STALLING (石江山), associate professor of English literature at the University of Oklahoma, is the author of *Poetics of Emptiness: Transformations of Asian Thought in American Poetry* (Fordham University Press, 2011) and a co-editor (with Lucas Klein) of Ernest Fenollosa's *The Chinese Written Character as a Medium for Poetry: A Critical Edition* (Fordham University Press, 2010). He is the author of two books of poetry, *Grotto Heaven* (Chax, 2010) and *Yíngēlìshī* (Counterpath, 2011), and is the translator of *Winter Sun: Poetry by Shi Zhi* (University of Oklahoma, 2012). He is the co-founder and editor of the magazine *Chinese Literature Today (CLT),* editor of the CLT Book Series (University of Oklahoma Press), and deputy director of the Center for Study of China's Literature Abroad at Beijing Normal University.

AO WANG (王敖) received his PhD in Chinese literature from Yale University in 2008, and is currently a professor at Wesleyan University. He is the author of several books of poetry, including *Quatrains and Legends* (Writer's Press, 2007), winner of the prestigious Anne Gao Poetry Prize. He translates contemporary Chinese poetry and also translates poetry from English to Chinese, including Wallace Stevens's *Harmonium.*

AFAA M. WEAVER (蔚雅风) will soon publish his twelfth collection of original poetry in 2013, *The Government of Nature* (University of Pittsburgh Press, 2013). He studied translation at Brown University, where in 1987 he earned an MFA. He began studying Mandarin Chinese formally in 2002. In 2004–2005 he completed the intermediate-level course in Mandarin at Taipei Language Institute. He holds an endowed chair at Simmons College in Boston, Massachusetts.

New Cathay: Contemporary Chinese Poetry is part of

THE POETS IN THE WORLD SERIES

a Harriet Monroe Poetry Institute project supporting research
and publication of poetry and poetics from around the world and
highlighting the importance of creating a space for poetry in local
communities in the United States.

CURRENT PUBLICATIONS

Katharine Coles, HMPI inaugural director

Poetry and New Media: A Users' Guide
report of the Poetry and New Media Working Group
(Harriet Monroe Poetry Institute, 2009)

Blueprints: Bringing Poetry into Communities
edited by Katharine Coles
(University of Utah Press, 2011)

Code of Best Practices in Fair Use for Poetry
created with American University's Center for Social Media and
Washington College of Law, 2011

Ilya Kaminsky, HMPI director, 2010–2013

Open the Door: How to Excite Young People About Poetry
edited by Jesse Nathan, Dominic Luxford, and Dorothea Lasky
(McSweeney's)

The Strangest of Theatres: Poets Writing Across Borders
edited by Jared Hawkley, Susan Rich, and Brian Turner
(McSweeney's)

FORTHCOMING PUBLICATIONS

Pinholes in the Night: Essential Poems from Latin America
edited by Raúl Zurita and Forrest Gander
(Copper Canyon Press)

On the Road
edited by Eliot Weinberger
(Open Letter Books)

Something Indecent: Poems Recommended by Eastern European Poets
edited by Valzhyna Mort
(Red Hen Press)

An Anthology of Anglophone Poetry
edited by Catherine Barnett (Tupelo Press)

Fifteen Iraqi Poets
edited by Dunya Mikhail
(New Directions Publishing)

A Star by My Head: Twelve Swedish Poets
edited and translated by Malena Mörling and Jonas Ellerström
(Milkweed Editions)

See our complete backlist at www.tupelopress.org